MASTER
your
MINDSET

9 Keys to Gaining Control Over the Mess in Your Head

SHELLY C. CORAY

Copy Editing: Evelyn Jeffries

Design & Photography: Chelsea Lewis

Printed in the United States of America

ISBN: 978-0692627044

For Jimmy and our littles

You were to FLY!

Vom

♡ Shelly

for you to here

THE 9 KEYS

Foreward -VII

Acknowledgements - - - - - - - - - - - - - - - - - IX

Preface - XI

1 - Do the Work -1

2 - Take Responsibility - - - - - - - - - - - - - - -9

3 - Train your Brain - - - - - - - - - - - - - - - - - 23

4 - Create Habits - - - - - - - - - - - - - - - - - - - 39

5 - Develop Gratitude - - - - - - - - - - - - - - - - 47

6 - Build Your Confidence - - - - - - - - - - - - - 53

7 - Choose Courage - - - - - - - - - - - - - - - - - 65

8 - Change Your Perspective - - - - - - - - - - - 75

9 - Develop an Outward Mindset - - - - - - - - - 81

The Wrap Up - 91

FOREWORD

Perception

It is commonly said, "We don't see things as they are; we see things as we are." From subtle to severe, what we see is generally filtered through colored lenses—lenses that have been tainted, altered, colored by our experience.

Perception is how we see. How we frame what we see is our mindset. Perception, right or wrong, clear or colored, creates our mindset. A friend once told me that everything we experience is as if it is projected on the inside of a box. Our mindset is that projection, and it is all we have. We can get out of our box, but the instructions for escape are printed on the outside of our box. That's why we need coaches – those who can read the instructions to us.

You are never wrong about how you feel. How you feel is always completely consistent with your mindset. If you want to feel differently, start working on your mindset. Our circumstances just don't matter as much as we think they do.

One of my favorite things about being a psychologist is that I get to illuminate the obvious. Think about that for a minute. I actually get paid to tell people things they already know, or show them what they already see. But sometimes the obvious is unnoticed. Like the feeling of your shirt – can you feel it now? Sure you can feel it – it is obvious. But that obvious feeling was unnoticed right up until the time you read my words asking if you can feel it. Master Your Mindset is a quick peek into your own mind. Shelly has a way of presenting the obvious in a way that is not only psychologically sound and accurate, but also refreshingly authentic and immediately applicable. Pay attention! She's reading the instructions to you.

Shelly Coray is a coach in every sense of the word. She can't win the game for you, but here she is on the sidelines cheering for you with an unquestioned commitment to the outcome of the game and a clear vision of what it takes for you, the hero and champion of the game, to win. Combine that with the passion of a devoted mother, and this is one coach you absolutely want to have on your side. Master Your Mindset helps you know where to start. As you Master Your Mindset, you take control over your own life, move beyond the messes, and create and live the life you love on purpose.

Paul H. Jenkins, Ph.D.
Positivity Psychologist
www.drpauljenkins.com

ACKNOWLEDGMENTS

As a little girl I dreamed of writing a book. I always thought it would be about things I learned in my life, but I hated writing and from my limited perception, I couldn't even imagine having anything valuable to share.

A few years ago God nudged me to start the Master Your Mindset Coaching Program as a way to help Mompreneurs learn how to have greater success in their business and home life. As I would sit down to prepare for our coaching calls the words would begin to flow, and in a matter of minutes I had captured pages and pages of content that I felt compelled to share. It came easily because it came straight from my heart and my head. It was all the knowledge I had gained over several years of researching, training, athletic coaching, and searching for the answers to the mess in my own head.

As people continued to ask me to share the knowledge I had gained I realized I needed a way to get it into more hands. I wanted so badly for every person to understand that they have power to change their thoughts, and therefore change their behaviors and their results.

This book has been a year of blood, sweat, and tears. Special thanks goes out to the many mentors, family, friends, and fellow speakers who continued to prod and sometimes pull me along through the journey.

This book would not be what it is without the genius of Chelsea Lewis, who spent several days designing, editing, photographing, formatting, and cheerleading so this project could be in your hands.

Evelyn Jeffries, dear friend and brilliant editor, thanks for believing in me and telling me that my message was worth sharing. Your support gave me the hope I needed to push through.

The biggest thank you goes to my sweetheart and biggest fan,

Jimmy. Without your countless hours sharing the "mom" responsibilities and many more hours being the behind-the-scenes business man, this book would still be sitting in my head. Your confidence and love have helped me see who I can become.

Last, I thank a loving God who has allowed me to learn the hard way, and given me opportunities to grow and become so I can share my story with others.

PREFACE

Master Your Mindset was born from my own journey to gain control over the mess in my head. As a teenager I was often told that my thoughts had power — a power that I could harness and use for good; a power that could change my whole outlook and my results. But no one ever told me how the power worked or how to apply it in my life.

As a high school athlete and competitive performer I used strategies such as visualization and positive statements on a daily basis, although I didn't really know what they were or how they worked. I just knew that they worked. I was getting great results in my performing, but I was really struggling in athletics and personal confidence.

I started to wonder what made the champion athletes different from me. I showed up to practice every day just like them. I worked hard, was open to learning, wanted it badly, and respected my coaches. But many of them were having great success while I was stuck in mediocre land. I knew that my body had more to give, but I didn't know how to dig deep and retrieve it. And I had no idea how to deal with the massive amounts of fear that overcame me every time I had to compete. Sometimes the fear was so overwhelming that I refused to try new things, or I'd quit altogether. I didn't know how to break the mental barriers I had created for myself and didn't know where else to turn, so I gave up — on dreams, goals, and ambitions.

As I got older I continued to struggle with bouts of depression and anxiety and didn't know how to "snap out of it." Only now it wasn't just affecting my athletics — it was also affecting every other aspect of my life. But that is a story for another book.

For the past 16 years I have continued to be heavily involved in high school athletics as a coach and manager and have watched other kids dealing with the same issues I have. I promised myself and God that if He would help me learn how to conquer the mindset game, I would spend my life teaching others how to do the same. I can't sit back and watch youth (or other adults, for that matter) give up on the things that are so important to them because they can't control the mess in their heads.

After years of studying, attending seminars, certifications, and hands on application with my clients and athletes and especially myself, I have compiled what I have learned in the hope that some other soul won't have to wait as long as I did to win at the mind game and harness the power that can change their world. May that person be you!

KEY # 1:

DO THE WORK

"Success doesn't come to you. You go to it."
Marva Collins

I was once taught that if I wanted something bad enough, thought about it all the time, visualized it, looked at pictures of it, and then sat and waited, it would come to me. I kept thinking one day I would walk out into the garage and it would be there — a bright red shiny sports car. But alas, all that greets me when I step out the door is a worn but trusty minivan. So what went wrong? Didn't I want it bad enough? Maybe I wasn't clear enough in my desire? What I later learned was missing was an essential piece to getting what you want — the part where you do the work.

I want to let you in on a secret. I like to call it "The Success Triangle."

SKILL SET

On one leg of the triangle is SKILL SET.

SKILL SET is the group of actual skills I need to succeed. These are habits, systems, programs, tools, etc. Let's use an example: most moms want success in keeping the dishes clean. So let's talk through the skills, tools, and systems needed to keep the sink empty and the cupboards full.

The system to keeping the dishes clean might start with the kids unloading the dishwasher before they go to school. Mom continues to load it all day immediately after each meal so the sink stays empty; then Dad runs the dishwasher before he goes to bed so the dishes will be clean in the morning. As long as we all do our part in the system, the system works and the dishes stay clean.

The tools I may use to do this are a great scrub brush, dishwasher detergent that works, and an organized place to put the dishes once they are clean. And as long as I have learned the skill of rinsing the food off the dishes before loading them, I have everything I need for success in keeping the sink empty and the cupboards full. All these things fall onto the skill set leg of the triangle.

MINDSET

The second leg is MINDSET. This means my thinking is supportive of the systems and habits I have created. If I haven't created a belief that keeping the dishes done makes my day goes smoother, or if I don't believe that the chaos in the sink usually brings chaos everywhere else, then why would I ever bother to follow my system and do the dishes? I wouldn't even realize why it was important for me to keep up on the dishes if it hadn't bothered me or caused some discontent.

I have noticed that if I am struggling to follow the system I have in place, it is often because I don't have the right mindset and motivation supporting the system. I hear from so many people, and have experienced it myself, that one of our biggest challenges is being consistent with our systems. Whether it is a meal plan, doing homework with the kids, exercising, or working from home, it's usually not a problem with our system. It's usually a problem with our mindset. Because we don't recognize it, we move through system after system trying to find one that suits our needs. While I do believe that we each may need a different system that is compatible with our personalities and family circumstances, I think too often we blame the system for our lack of mindset concerning the issue.

ACTION

If you find yourself in the right mindset and having a system you love, but are still not achieving the results you desire, you may have a problem with the third leg of the triangle, which is ACTION, or actually doing the work. So often we believe that if we have the right tools and the right mindset things will just fall into place, like the red sports car in the garage. Guess what? Things don't work unless we do!

The other day I was at an event where a raffle was taking place. After one of the women won a prize she stated, "I manifested that!" This statement has always made me chuckle just a bit. While there is truth in the statement "You get what you think about," if she hadn't actually bought her tickets and put them in the jar, she would not have "manifested" anything. So while I absolutely tell my clients to focus on what they want, I don't tell them to do it from the sidelines of the game or in their Lazy Boy chair. You can't score the basket from the sidelines. You must be an active participant in the game itself. You've got to be DOING something if you want results.

Back to our dishes analogy. If you really know and believe that keeping the dishes clean makes for a better day in your home, and you have built a system for your family to follow, but refuse to actually do the work, the system will fail every time! A triangle isn't a triangle with only two legs. It's just an angle, created by two lines that will never meet again.

When you can consistently put all three legs of this triangle together, you have a concrete recipe for success.

APPLY THE SUCCESS TRIANGLE

So how does the Success Triangle play into Mastering your Mindset? It's not just on the Mindset Leg of the triangle. Think of this triangle in the context of having success developing the mindset you desire.

First, you need the tools and systems, step-by-step processes that change the neuropathways in your brain and help you gain greater control over your thoughts, and thus your results. You will learn many of these throughout the course of this book.

Second, you need to develop the mindset or desire to actually change. You must have an idea of how mastering your mindset will change your life and believe in that process. And since you are reading this book, you probably already have a desire to do that (unless you are friends or family who are reading out of duty or curiosity. Wink, wink).

And last, you must actually do the work. Some of that work will be writing, listening, and reading. Much of it will be conscious decision-making to reroute your thought patterns. At times this process can be painful. But in this situation, pain is an indicator of growth and progress.

This work requires you to be brutally honest with yourself. Nothing will change if you don't acknowledge the behaviors and thoughts that are keeping you stuck. And again, sometimes the honesty is painful.

But it is also liberating. When you realize that you have power to change things you once believed were far beyond your control, you feel like you can conquer the world. Taking that step to become accountable for your circumstances and results will give you greater power and confidence to really have the life of your dreams, filled with peace, joy, and love.

WHERE ARE YOU NOW?

Take some time to honestly answer the following questions. There is power in writing it down, so grab a pen and paper.

1. What does my life feel like right now? (Home, family, relationships, business, etc.)

2. What is my mindset like? Positive or negative? What is my self-talk like?

3. How long have I been in this place?

4. What does it feel like to be here? (Comfortable, uncomfortable, easy, boring, discontent, happy, disappointing etc.)

5. Where do I want to be? What does my ideal life feel like? How do I want to be mentally? Physically? Emotionally? Spiritually?

6. What does being that kind of person or having that life feel like?

7. What is stopping me from being that person or having that life?

8. What changes would I have to make to become that person or have that life?

9. On a scale of 1-10, 1 being not at all, how committed am I to making those changes?

10. What is my motivation for change? (Not what I think it should be, but what it really is.)

If you had to rate your life on a scale of one to ten, ten being exuberantly happy and feeling overwhelming peace, where would you say you are right now? I know that this can vary from day to day, so just do an average over the last few weeks or months.

If you could increase that number even by 1, how would your

life be different?

In this world of instant gratification we want something that will fix it all right now and make it all better. We want our life to be a 10 all the time, and we want it yesterday. I've looked for that answer, the magic quick fix, and it doesn't exist. I'm sorry.

I know that the things you are going to learn over the next few pages create a path to this place of peace, hope, fulfillment, and joy. It takes work, patience, persistence, faith, trust, a little bit of pixie dust, work, and more work. If you are willing to put in the consistent effort, your life can change and you can move on to the amazing future God has waiting for you.

Let me give you some advice that I learned the hard way. Your past, is just that—your past. Refer to it for evaluation only! Not to beat yourself up, but to look back and say, what can I learn from that situation or circumstance? How might I do things differently this time around so I get different results? How did it feel when I did it last time and what can I do to make it feel differently this time? Again, we aren't looking backward to place judgment on ourselves or to blame ourselves. Look backward only to evaluate what happened so you can create something better.

Let's focus on your future. What do you want to create? You just wrote about the ideal you, or your ideal life. Take a moment to imagine what that looks and feels like. Now, what would it take to get there, or what would it take to increase even just one number? Maybe you know, maybe you don't. Over the next few chapters you will learn what it will take and how to do it, to bump that number up, even just one, hopefully more. But I can't stress enough how important it is to DO THE WORK!

Stephen R. Covey states: "If we [want] to change the situation, we first [have] to change ourselves. And to change ourselves effectively, we first [have] to change our perceptions."[1]

1   Stephen R. Covey, The 7 Habits of Highly Effective People (New York: Simon & Schuster, 1989)

(handwritten margin note: You can't change the past. Just learn from it.)

If you want different results you must start DOING things differently. The definition of insanity is doing the same thing over and over again hoping to get a different result. And maybe you feel a bit of insanity in your life right now.

To start doing things differently you must start SEEING things differently. This is where Mastering Your Mindset starts.

Note: At the end of each chapter you will find a "Gut Check." This is an opportunity to look inward and see how you are doing with each topic. Sometimes gut checks are painful, but push forward anyway. Remember that mastering your mindset doesn't happen overnight.

KEY # 2:

TAKE RESPONSIBILITY

"The price of greatness is responsibility."
Winston Churchill

ARE YOU RESPONSIBLE?

When I ask my students and athletes if they consider themselves responsible they often reply "Yes." Then I ask them to define what that means. The most common responses I hear are:

"I do what I am told."

"I get to school and work on time."

"People can count on me."

"I pay my bills and clean my room."

"Yep," I tell them, "that's what I always thought responsible meant, too." And it does.

The dictionary states that being responsible is "having an obligation to do something, or having control over or care for someone, as part of one's job or role."

I agree with that definition, and to that extent I would say that I was a really responsible person and so are many of the individuals I have worked with, including you. But I learned a new definition that changed my life.

One day I was reading in Jack Canfield's book The Success Principles and a light bulb went on. He tells of being asked by an early mentor if he took 100% responsibility for his life. Unsure of what was being implied, he cautiously answered "I think so."

His mentor replied, "This is a yes or no question, young man. You either do or you don't." Still unsure how to respond, Jack was soon asked another question: "Have you ever blamed anyone for any circumstance in your life? Have you ever complained about anything?"[1]

Of course, all of us can answer yes to that question if we take a minute to think about it. We are surrounded at every turn by excuses, blame, justification, and even lying. In my 16 years of involvement in high school track and field programs I have heard just about everything.

"Coach, I didn't run my best because of the rain."

"Coach, it's too cold to get a personal record today."

"I'm sorry, Coach, I got a really bad handoff from so-and-so and it held me up."

"She dropped the baton, Coach. What was I supposed to do?"

I have even heard some of these same excuses come out of the mouths of well-meaning coaches and parents:

"Now, we don't expect your best because of the weather."

"It's pretty hard to have a good race on this kind of track."

"That starter stinks. He totally messed up your start for you."

1   Jack Canfield, The Success Principles (New York: HarperCollins Publishers, 2015)

The list could go on and on. And I used to believe many of the same justifications.

That section of Jack's book hit me like a ton of bricks. I started evaluating all the things I blamed on others. I had learned to believe that I was a victim in this life — that life happened to me and I didn't have much say about the outcome. It was my duty to endure all that came my way and try to do it happily. And because I believed I didn't have a choice, I always had someone or something to blame for how I got where I was — unhappy, broke, and lost. And believe me, my list of excuses was a mile long. It didn't matter what things affected my results; they were never my fault. Because I perceived life as always involving things outside my control, I felt helpless to change my results.

The truth is, these are all just justifications we use to avoid taking accountability. They keep us safe and comfortable, but they also keep us failing at having the life we were designed to live.

QUIT PLAYING THE BLAME GAME

How many of you blame your parents, teachers, or childhood bullies for your low self- esteem? I am not excusing the actions of people who may have said or done things that you chose to let hurt you, but blaming them does nothing to help you move forward. It just gives you an excuse to stay where you are, to make no change.

When you can look at your past, recognize it for what it is — the past — and choose to move forward without any blame, excuse, or justification, then your life can start to improve.

I will be totally honest, I have spent a lot of time blaming people in my past for my own struggles with love and confidence. For many years I used that as a crutch, to keep me where I was, because taking responsibility for my own actions was painful and challenging. But I am not alone and neither are you.

A few years ago I was listening as a dear friend struggled with her own self-worth. She kept saying, "If my Mom would only treat me a certain way, I would know she loved me and then I would love myself." I listened patiently as she continued to blame her Mom for her own feelings of rejection and insecurity. After some time of talking in circles and lots of tears, I finally got the courage to ask her a question.

"So what if your Mom never treats you like that? Does that mean you are not a worthwhile individual? Does that mean that God doesn't love you? Does that mean that you don't have value in this life or the next?" She looked at me stunned as she pondered my questions. I continued:

"At some point you are going to have to start taking responsibility for your own happiness and quit making it contingent on other people. You are going to have to quit blaming others for your unhappiness if you are ever going to be truly happy."

This isn't easy in a world where it has become commonplace to drop the blame in someone else's lap. But it is possible.

BLAME KEEPS YOU FROM GROWING

I use another analogy with my athletes that seems to hit home. Two boys, Johnny and Steve, are playing on the same basketball team. The game is tied with 10 seconds to go. The referee makes an obvious wrong call that gives the other team a chance to win the game, which they do.

In the locker room we hear Johnny: "That stupid ref! What a bad call! He lost the game for us!"

Then we hear another voice, that of Steve, saying: "We lost by two points. I know the call was bad, but if I had hit even one more of my shots we would have tied. If I hadn't slacked off on defense during the first half, we could have stopped one more of their baskets. I missed three foul shots. If I had made them, we would have won the game."

During the next week Steve works hard to improve on the skills that he lacked during the game, while Johnny continues to complain and blame the ref. His skills don't increase because he sees no need to get better.

At Friday's game, Steve makes all of his foul shots, plays intense defense, and becomes a more valuable player for the team, while Johnny's skills and attitude stay the same.

As a coach or parent, which child would you rather have to work with? Which would you prefer to BE? Would you rather feel like Steve, who is continuing to grow and increase his skill level, or would you rather walk around bitter and angry like Johnny? It's entirely up to you.

CHOOSE YOUR RESPONSE

Often in this world we believe that there is an event and then there is the outcome. But I believe, as Jack Canfield shares, that there is actually an equation to our outcome:

$$\text{Event} + \text{Response} = \text{Outcome}$$
$$\text{or}$$
$$E+R=O.[2]$$

The event happens, then we choose how we respond to it, and those things together equal our outcome. You can choose your response to the event, and that makes all the difference.

Stephen R. Covey gives us a little different look at the word "responsibility" in his book The 7 Habits of Highly Effective People. He states that when you break down the word it becomes "response able," or having the ability to choose your response.[3] I love that definition. You truly do have the ability to choose your response and therefore affect your outcome.

A few years ago, I had a young man in one of my classes who had been in an accident in which he had fractured his skull. He

2   Ibid.
3   Covey, op. cit.

was in a wheelchair and neck brace and was struggling to see how his situation could be positive. His doctors told him he might never walk again and would be confined to the chair for the rest of his life. He was living in a toxic situation and was feeling extremely doubtful that his life would ever become what he had once hoped.

During our class we covered E+R=O, and discussed how he could choose the response to the event. We talked about what he really wanted in life, his hopes for the future, and what it would take to get there. He shared his dreams of being a high school teacher and coach, of traveling around the states working for the Red Cross, and of having a wife and family. He was afraid none of it would ever be possible if he could never walk again.

Over the course of our several-week program, he slowly learned that he had control over his outcome by choosing how to respond to his situation. He chose to exercise that control by studying all he could about his future profession while he was confined to the wheelchair. He read books, did research, listened to classes, and did his course work.

Within a few weeks he was regaining his strength and was soon able to walk again. He applied for a position in a school district helping youth, volunteered as a coach, and moved away from a toxic situation at home.

Now, two years later, he is thriving, learning, and growing. He attends college where he is learning to become a teacher. And he now has a paid coaching job, a dream come true. Things aren't perfect and he still faces many health challenges, but he is on his way to making his dream life happen because he chose a different response — to be the hero instead of the victim.

Choosing a positive response can mean the difference between a life of success and happiness or a life of bitterness and sadness.

DO YOU LIVE IN VICTIMVILLE?

Another common way we struggle with responsibility is victimhood. Do you often feel like a victim, and want others to know it? I often see this come out in an ugly form when we start comparing stories with our friends.

It's the "Who has the worst pregnancy story?" in which women tell how their story is far worse than anyone else's. I have been there, done that, and won the contest many times.

But why do we thrive on victimhood? For most of us we wear victimhood as a badge of honor. "Look at all I have suffered!" "I am the martyr here and I want to be noticed for my sacrifice!"

Until we can quit being the victim in our own story, we will never have the life we really desire because victimhood keeps us stuck. We gain such gratification from the attention we get as a victim that we refuse to step up into another role — that of the hero of our story!

Sometimes listening to others' opinions and internalizing them keeps you as a resident in Victimville. How many times do you replay what others have said to you and use it as an excuse to stay where you are? It happens all the time. But we have the power to rise above the criticism and become something really significant.

Think about Michael Jordan, the greatest basketball player of all time. After being cut from his high school basketball team, he went home, locked himself in his room, and cried. He went on to win six NBA championships, become the NBA MVP five times and an NBA All-star four times. What if he had played the victim card and listened when they told him he wasn't good enough?

If Michael can let go of it, so can you! You are NOT a victim in this mortal journey, but a champion if you choose to be one. LET IT GO!

* LIVE IN THE 90'S

Speaker, author, world record holder, and my personal mentor Brad Barton shares an idea in his book Beyond Illusions about our response. He states: "Life is 10% what happens to me and 90% how I respond to it."

"What happens," he asks, "when I accept greater responsibility for my day? My focus shifts from what happens to me (the 10%) to my vast ability to perceive, interpret, consider and thoughtfully respond (the 90%) and I become more powerful as a result. I then set my own pace, run my own race, and obtain the prize—freedom. When we focus on the 10% (what happens to us) and just sit in it, bemoaning our fate and not moving into the 90% (what we can do about it), we give what happens to us much more weight than it deserves. We then remain helpless, hopeless victims of circumstance. We lose the greatest prize of all-freedom."[4]

So, are you going to live in the 90% of what you can control and become the champion, or are you going to focus on the 10% and stay stuck, void of hope and most importantly, freedom.

EXCUSES ARE JUST LIES

Sam Silverstein wrote in his book No More Excuses that an excuse is a story you tell yourself to sell to yourself—and then try to sell to others.[5] Some of us, including myself are master salesmen.

I hadn't realized how much I used excuses for everything until one day I was headed to a meeting out of town. I ran to our print shop to pick up something for the meeting and met a friend in the parking lot. I stayed to visit with her for several minutes, anxiously watching my clock. I was on a tight schedule and did not really have time for our friendly chat. But I stayed anyway.

4   Brad Barton, Beyond Illusions (Brooksville, FL: Kat Ranch Publishing, 2011)
5   Sam Silverstein, No More Excuses

Once on the road, I hit traffic that I had not anticipated and was even later for the meeting. As I walked in from the parking lot my mind was reeling with all the excuses I could give for being late that took the responsibility off of me.

"I hit heavy traffic."

"I had to take care of some things at our store."

"I got stuck in a conversation I couldn't get out of."

My mind was reeling with which excuse would sell the easiest until I realized what I was doing.

Lying.

By the time I stepped off the elevator I decided I was going to be honest and not give any excuses. I simply stated that I was sorry I was late. Then I decided that next time, I would leave a little earlier to accommodate for traffic, I would tell my friend I didn't have time to chat but that I would call her, and I would take care of things at the store the day before. Taking responsibility not only kept me from being a liar, but it helped me see what I could do next time to avoid the same mistake.

Many of us use the excuse sales techniques all the time on our children or others.

Several years ago I heard an older gentleman chew out my generation for using the phrase "Just a second."

"It's never just one second," he claimed. "You are lying!"

I remember how that hit me. And now I have a child who takes everything I say literally and calls me out on it. I had to change my reply when she kept saying, "Mom, it's been more than a second."

I used to say things like, "Honey, I can't help you right now. I need to finish this chapter." And that wasn't the truth. The truth sounded a little more like "I don't want to stop right now and help you. I want to finish what I am doing." But that always seemed harsh.

What I finally learned to say was something more like "Honey, I really want to finish this chapter before I stop. Can you give me 30 minutes and I will be able to spend some time with you uninterrupted?"

I soon realized that once I started being more honest in what I said to others, I started being more intentional and integral. And with integrity comes strength. Zig Ziglar said: "With integrity you have nothing to fear, since you have nothing to hide. With integrity you will do the right thing so you will have no guilt. With fear and guilt removed you are free to be and do your best."[6]

This small change of being completely honest with my children may seem like an insignificant change, but it gave me the opportunity to have 100% integrity all of the time and let go of the guilt and fear I had gained from telling white lies to my children and others.

TAKING RESPONSIBILITY BRINGS POWER

"Truly effective people admit fault when they've made a mistake. They inevitably gain strength by making that admission. Weak people, on the other hand, usually try to attach fault for a problem to someone or something outside of their control, and they always seem to become a little weaker as a result."
Sam Silverstein

A few weeks ago I was facilitating a discussion with a group of women in the "Rise Up" program. We were taking on a challenge of "No Excuses" for an entire week. The feedback surprised me. One of the women stated that she felt more strength when she refused to offer an excuse when she had made a mistake. Somehow it made the mistake seem less painful. She couldn't explain

6   Zig Ziglar, podcast

it, but as we have already talked about, there is power in being fully integral, even in small matters. The adversary gets a swift kick in the pants when we won't buy into his lies and methods of shading the truth. And when he is no longer gaining ground with us, we are filled with Divine power that gives us extra strength.

ARE YOU BECOMING?

So many of us want to make a difference in this life. We want to do great things and make this world a better place. But we often get stuck wondering how to do that. We believe that if we just have enough money, or the right resources we could do all we ever dreamed. We buy in to the idea that if our reality was just a little different, we could be what we really want to be.

Doug Nielson, author of the book Take Life by the Helm, states: "As tough as things can get, difficult circumstances simply aren't a good enough excuse for us NOT to fulfill our dreams."[7]

So many of us on this earth are walking around using tough times as an excuse to play small, or to not become who we are designed to be. And we often believe that if we could have what we want to have, and do what we were meant to do, then we would be the person we were created to be.

But we have it all backwards. If we will first be who we want and need to be, then we will, by default, do what we need to do to have what we want to have.

I had a conversation with a young divorced man once. He was discouraged that since his divorce he was unable to find any women whom he had an interest in dating. He started to describe the type of women he was hoping to find. After listening to his checklist, I quietly asked him how he was doing at being the person he described. He looked at me stunned: "Why would I

7   Doug Nielson, Take Life By the Helm (Ogden, UT: DNC Publishing, 2014)

need to be that person? That is what I am looking for, not who I am." At the time he was making choices that were leading him farther and farther away from the kind of woman he wanted to marry. I asked him, "Do you think a woman like that is going to be attracted to the person you are right now? If you want to find the right woman, be the right man."

Are you focusing first on what you want to become instead of what you want to have? Are you using your life circumstances as an excuse to not become?

Tell someone like Nick Vujicic, who was born without any arms and legs, that he can't do something to make a difference, that he can't live his dreams. He will say you are lying. Nick is a powerful speaker who travels around the world sharing his message that being a victim gets us nowhere.

Albert Einstein's teachers told him he would never amount to much. He wasn't even able to speak until he was four years old. What if he had listened? Where would we be without his breakthroughs in physics?

I love this poem. It says it like it really is.

"Build a better world," said God.

And I asked, "How?

The world is such a vast place and so complicated now.

I am small and useless.

What can I do?"

God in all His wisdom said, "Just build a better you."

GUT CHECK

Do you blame others for the circumstances you find yourself in? Do you make excuses or complain? Are you willing to step up and take responsibility in your response to events or circumstances in which you find yourself? Are you willing to focus on becoming the best you possible? If you are, then be prepared to move out of Victimville and Mediocre Land and move into a life of success, growth, and happiness.

KEY # 3:

TRAIN YOUR BRAIN

"Whatever we plant in our subconscious mind and nourish with repetition and emotion will eventually become our reality."
Earl Nightingale

Let me wow you with some numbers. Our brain's capacity is pretty incredible. It is estimated to have 85 billion neuron cells. And each neuron forms about 1,000 connections to other neurons that have the ability to store 3-4 million bits of information. These neuron cells process and transmit information through electrical and chemical signals. When these neurons connect together they form neural networks or patterns.[1]

For every movement our body makes, every thought we think, or anything we see, smell, taste, hear, or touch, our brain creates a neuron chain or neural pathway and stores this in our brain's computer.

If you were to build a computer large enough to do the work your brain does it would be larger than the state of Texas — two

---

1   Susan Gardener, The Winner's Creed (self-published seminar workbook)

stories high — and would put off enough heat to keep the entire world warm. Your brain has amazing power!

Harnessing that power becomes the challenge. How do you program your brain to help you do things differently? First you must understand the functions of your brain.

HOW DECISIONS ARE MADE

Imagine your brain as a ship. On your ship you have the captain, who represents the conscious mind; the crew, who represent the subconscious mind; and the ship, that represents your body or the vessel that houses the crew and captain.

The captain has a very important job on the ship. He is the one and only person on the ship who can make decisions. Making a decision is a four-step process for the conscious mind.

First, your conscious mind perceives a situation.

Second, it associates that situation with other situations like it in the past.

Third, it evaluates the associations to determine what option would be best.

Fourth, it decides on a course of action.

In order to make these decisions the captain, or conscious mind, has to have access to some information. He has help gathering this information, the five senses; Sight, Sound, Touch, Smell and Taste. They are picking up on everything going on around him. They gather the information, approximately two million bits every second, and give it to the captain's first mate, the Reticular Activating System (RAS), who sorts through the data and separates it into two categories: Valuable and/or Threatening, and Everything Else. The RAS presents the captain, or conscious mind, with the valuable and/or threatening information he needs to make decisions that would be best for the ship, then sends "everything else" to the crew, or subconscious mind, and tells them to store it in the deep files of the ship, because they might need it later.

THE FUNCTIONS OF THE SUBCONSCIOUS

Let's talk about the crew of our ship. We all know that they are the ones really running the ship. They do all the work, they just need to be told what to do by the captain. The crew has some functions that have become habits, like keeping the ship clean, putting up the sails, making the meals, etc. The crew also has set tasks that they take care of daily that may change or are not habits — just whatever the captain asks. Your subconscious works the same way. It has a few primary functions, just like the crew, that it does out of habit. And it also has other functions it does on command from your conscious mind.

The first function of your subconscious mind is to keep the automatic functions of the physical and mental processes of your body going, like breathing, heartbeat, blood circulation, and food digestion, without you consciously thinking about them. You are usually not aware of these things unless something out of the ordinary happens, such as not getting enough oxygen, or your digestive system not working properly. When something isn't working right this function is brought out of the subconscious to your conscious mind so you can deal with it and fix the problem.

The second function of your subconscious mind is to record and store all the information your five senses gather. It stores these as memories and experiences that you can draw on at a later date if you have a use for them. These become important when your conscious mind needs to make a decision but needs to relate the information to something. For instance, you know to take an umbrella with you when it rains because you have been in other rain storms and have gotten wet. When the conscious mind sees the rain, it goes back through the "files" to see what other experiences were like what it sees now, and then uses those experiences to guide this current decision to take an umbrella. It also uses these files when it is working on achieving goals, which we will talk about later.

Another function of the subconscious is to help your conscious mind focus on the things only it can do by taking over anything that has a set process. When your subconscious knows that you follow the same pattern every time, it creates a neural pathway to follow so that at some point it takes over that task for you and you no longer have to use conscious energy to do it. Some of these tasks include things like tying your shoes, writing your name, eating, driving, walking etc. If you had to think through the steps of tying your shoes every time you put them on, you would be wasting time and that drives your subconscious crazy. It wants you to be as efficient as possible! Research shows that 40% of all your actions fall into the category of being run by the subconscious. That is great news if you have programmed it correctly. But often people have fallen into patterns that don't serve them.

CREATING PATTERNS

There are two ways you can program patterns into your subconscious; physical repetition or visual imagination. What's crazy is it can't tell the difference between physical action and imagined thoughts. And once you have done or thought something repeatedly, the subconscious picks up on the fact that it has traveled down the neural pathway over and over and it takes care of it for you. This is a huge advantage to you, if you know how to use it.

Athletes call this muscle memory. It is the goal of an athlete to do the same motion so many times consciously (while thinking it through) that eventually the subconscious picks it up as a habit and takes it over so they can focus on other things. This is why visualization has been a long proven method of training for athletes and performers. Their bodies actually don't know whether they physically ran the hurdle race or just imagined it. But if it goes over that motion in the exact same way multiple times physically or visually, the subconscious creates the pathway and behaves accordingly.

This function of the subconscious is pretty amazing. Remember how the subconscious stores your memories and experiences? Because of what you just learned, you now know that your subconscious has the ability to remember and store an event or activity that is totally imagined. As long you make the memory very vivid it will remember it as real.

For example, when I was a young girl I remember having a family of skunks living in our back yard. They were so cute! I recall watching them follow my father around the yard. I can see that memory as if it happened yesterday. But when I ask my dad or siblings about it, they tell me I am making it up. I guess I did, but I must have painted such a vivid image that my subconscious believes it was true and has stored it as a real memory.

HOW YOUR SUBCONSCIOUS CAN HURT YOU

Why does information about how patterns and memories are stored matter? Remember how the conscious mind uses these memories when it is making decisions? What if you have programmed memories that affect your decision making negatively?

It has happened in my own life. I really want to learn to surf. But I keep imagining myself getting sucked under the water when I am not prepared and not having enough air. I have thought that scene over and over in my head until I have planted in my subconscious a belief that that is exactly what will happen if I go surfing. So when presented with the option to go, I turned it down.

Do you see how an imagined memory can affect your ability to do something you really want or need to do? And chances are, your imagined memory is based on a fear that may not even happen. But because of that memory, you may miss out on a great opportunity to do something you have always dreamed of.

This also explains how you almost always get what you think about in life. You have probably said or thought the phrase "I knew that was going to happen." And the truth is, you did know, because you thought about it so much that your subconscious made it your reality. This is why focusing on what you want to have happen instead of what you don't want to have happen is so important. Thinking over and over again of what isn't working only makes our subconscious think about that more and then it makes it happen.

THE SUBCONSCIOUS AND SELF-IMAGE

One of the most important functions of the subconscious is that it makes us act like we see ourselves to be. If you have always seen yourself as positive, outgoing, happy and optimistic, your subconscious will make you behave that way. If you don't behave the way you see yourself, you will feel discomfort.

This is how I explain my "belief-induced" depression. I knew who I really was inside and I thought about myself often as the person I really wanted to be, but I didn't live up to it. And I felt extreme discomfort. Not living up to your own value system or belief system can make you feel crazy, or depressed, or anxious!

Here is an example:

You have planted deeply in your subconscious an image of yourself as a fit and active person and incredible athlete. You see it vividly in your mind, running hurdles, blocking and attacking volleyballs, and swimming laps like a fish. You know in your mind what your body looks like, how you feel, and how much joy you have from being that person.

But, that is not your reality right now. And it is causing extreme discomfort every time you look in the mirror or get dressed. That is a good thing because it causes enough discontent that you will do the work to become what you imagine yourself to be.

Your subconscious will do what it can to help you. It will start sorting through all the deep files and see if it has anything that it can throw up to the conscious mind to help achieve the balance. You may start remembering workouts you really like, or friends you like to work out with. You may remember when you tried out a certain gym or a piece of equipment and got results. Maybe you will even remember some of the eating habits that worked before, or the eating plan put together by a nutritionist over 15 years ago and you will be able to go and find the book. It's amazing what the subconscious mind will store and bring up when you need it.

SELF-IMAGE AND SELF-TALK

Self-image is created by thinking something about yourself over and over until a strong neural pathway is created and your subconscious believes that the thought is your reality and makes you live up to it. Then starts the vicious self-talk cycle.

First you think a thought about yourself repeatedly. This generates your self-image. Your results or performance show what your self-image is because you must act accordingly or you feel crazy. If this cycle is negative it may look something like this.

Self-Talk: I tell myself I am bad at math.
Self-Image: I believe I really am bad at math.
Result: I score poorly on a math test.
Self-Talk: See, I told you that you were bad at math.
Self-Image: I have evidence that I really am bad at math, so I must be.
Result: I perform even more poorly at math.

The cycle continues to spiral downward unless you do something to change it. That change usually starts with your self-talk.

Self-Talk: I am a person who is progressing in my ability to do math.
Self-Image: I can do math!
Result: My math skills continue to grow.
Self-Talk: See, I told you that you could do math!
Self-Image: I am good at math.
Result: Math skills continue to grow and often become a strength instead of a weakness.

And the cool thing about the subconscious is that if you have told it that you are good at math, or that you have a goal to be good at math and give it a clear vision of what that looks like, it will start finding ways to make that a reality. It will sift through all the "deep files" to see if there are any answers there that can help you achieve the goal, like remembering about a tutor you once heard about, or finding an online study program, or a teacher who offered to help. If it doesn't find any answers it will start impressing you to look other places until you find the answer it is looking for. Boom!!! Isn't our brain amazing?!

OTHER IMPORTANT FACTS

Here are a few more points about the subconscious that are vital for you to know:

First, it doesn't know reality from imagination, good from bad, or past from future. So it won't filter things for you that might be dangerous and it doesn't understand humor so telling yourself you are just kidding doesn't work either.

Next, the subconscious doesn't understand the word "don't." It doesn't really have a picture associated with it. It only hears what you say or think after it. For instance, "Don't think about bunnies." What did you see? Bunnies of course. You probably didn't see a bunny with a red circle and a line through it, did you?

When you say things to yourself like "Don't fall" or "Don't slip on the ice" or "Don't touch the hot pan," your mind automatically sees pictures of you falling or slipping or touching something and getting burned. And those images, if you see them enough, tell your subconscious that those are patterns you want it to take over. And soon you find yourself falling often, or slipping, or getting burned.

Third, the subconscious is a goal-achieving machine! It doesn't make any decisions for itself so it uses all its energy on getting the goal, not setting it. Once it receives a clear message to go after something, it is 100% successful provided there isn't any interference! What interference might get in the way? Usually it's your negative self-talk, your doubt, and your fear.

How do you give your subconscious that clear message so it will help you get what you want?

GIVE IT TO ME IN ENGLISH

Speak its language. What is the language you understand the best? Mine is English, but I know a little Spanish and a word or two in Portuguese. If you want to be really clear with your communication, give it to me in English.

The primary language of the subconscious is images — pictures or movies. It understands other things as well, but nothing is as powerful as a vivid image. Using images or words that create images in your mind create the clearest and most powerful message to your subconscious.

Your subconscious loves details. It needs to engage as many of your senses as possible so it can connect with all the different stored files. Imagine what being in your movie reel would smell like, look like, taste like, sound like, and what you would be touching. Your subconscious also loves powerful emotion tied to the image. As you visualize, imagine what feelings you are experiencing, whether elation, joy, content, relief, or any others. I often use physical pictures to help me get my visualization started. Always imagine exactly what you want to have happen, not what you don't want to have happen.

VISUALIZATION

Visualization is nothing more than imagining something over and over again as if it's already happening, like watching a movie reel in your head.

Athletes and performers have used the power of visualization for years to help them train their brain to do something the same every time. As we have already talked about, our subconscious doesn't know whether we are really running over a flight of hurdles, or just imagining it, so there is much work we can do to create muscle memory without having to expend extra physical energy. I can imagine myself doing the skill, the dance, singing the song, or performing the routine perfectly multiple times a day. Once I have practiced that skill over and over again my body recognizes the pattern and my muscles fire the same every time. Once my muscles "remember" how to do the skill, my subconscious takes over, so I don't have to think about every detail of performing the skill and my conscious mind can now focus on the things that will change, such as weather, competition, surrounding, venues, etc. Every drill I do as an athlete to warm up or practice trains my body to behave in that pattern, as long as it is practiced correctly.

It used to be said, "Practice makes perfect." Now the saying is "Practice makes permanent." And this is why: whatever we do repeatedly, whether physically or in our imagination, becomes our reality.

We use visualization constantly in our world, but most of us just don't realize it or do it consciously.

Performers use forms of visualization constantly to "run" their number or routine in their mind. As a dancer I am constantly performing in my head so I will remember the steps. As a singer I am thinking through the words to songs and imagining myself singing them.

Visualization is also a powerful tool in mastering our mindset, for we can imagine ourselves seeing things a certain way, responding to a situation the way we want, or developing qualities or thought patterns we desire.

AFFIRMATIONS

> *"You are what you are and where you are by what you put into your mind. You can change what you are and where you are by changing what you put into your mind."*
> *Zig Ziglar*

An affirmation is a group of words or sentences that you read or think over and over so it gives your brain a chance to travel the new neural pathway multiple times. There are many one-line affirmations you can find on the internet, but I have found it much more effective to write a personal affirmation using phrases that trigger you.

How do you write an affirmation? Write what you want to have happen, in present tense as if it is already happening, using as much detail and emotion as you can. Using the words "I am" to start the statement gives your subconscious a command to become. Try to write things that engage as many of your senses as you can: what you hear, see, or smell. Include action words (ending in ing). Add "or something better" when applicable. Then pack it full of emotion. Spend time reading or thinking these phrases in your mind. This creates a new neural pathway. The more you go over that pathway, the quicker the new pattern develops. And remember, you can't write about things outside your control, such as other people.

Here's an example of a personal affirmation:

> *I am running a five-minute mile, or something better, confidently. I love the feeling of the ground under my feet and the sound of the other runners behind me. Running brings me great joy and my body loves being fit.*

GETTING OUT THE BACKHOE

I once asked a client how a hiking path was created. He said, "By walking down the path over and over." I then asked, "If you wanted to create that path faster, how would you do it?" His reply: "Use a backhoe."

Here's the backhoe of affirmations. It's called a "Byte" and it was created by Leo A. Weidner, author of The Slight Edge in Your Business and Personal Life.[2] I have found this to be one of the most successful ways to change a thought pattern very quickly. It's basically an affirmation on steroids.

> Step 1: At the top of a 3x5 card or small piece of paper write the one thing that you want to change in the form of a positive present tense statement (as if it was already reality). For example, if I wanted to get to bed by 10 pm every night I wouldn't write "Quit staying up late." I would write something more like "I go to bed every night by 10 pm."

> Step 2: Write what it feels like to be changed. Use as many emotion words as you can. State what it feels like physically, emotionally, mentally, etc. What are the benefits from this change? How are you better because you made this change? For example: "I wake up refreshed and ready to start the day. My body has renewed energy and has repaired itself from my workout and daily activities. My body has the energy it needs to do all that I ask of it."

> Step 3: Write what your motivation is for changing: "I want to be able to push my body at workouts so I can meet my goal of going to state. My body needs the rest to work harder so I can cut two seconds off my time."

2   Leo A. Weidner, The Slight Edge (Springville, UT: Cedar Fort, Inc., 2008)

Step 4: Carry the card with you at all times or put it in your pocket. Any time you feel you are thinking about staying up late, for whatever reason, pull out the card and read through it. This could happen several times a day. We want your brain to start a new neural pathway, forming a new habit. It may take time, but you have to actively train your brain to think differently.

CHOOSE YOUR PATH

Your mind can't focus on two conflicting thoughts at the same time. You have probably heard the phrase "You can't have faith and fear at the same time." It's true. Once you are on the path of fear you can't be on the other path of faith. But you can switch paths, even in the middle of the path. It just takes a conscious choice. If you find yourself on the negative path, consciously redirect it to the new path by reading or thinking the affirmation or byte over and over again. The more often you travel over the path, the quicker your brain will pick up on the message and make it a reality.

VISION BOARDS, GOAL JOURNALS

Because our subconscious loves images, vision boards and goal journals become powerful tools to train your subconscious on your goals. Placing images that represent your goals, desires, and dreams on a board or in a journal and looking at it often sends a powerful message to your brain. You can add words or phrases, emotions, deadlines, or other key components of your goals. Place it somewhere you will look at it several times a day. Spend time visualizing your goals happening as you look at the pictures.

IDEAL LIFEVISION

Another powerful tool I have used to communicate with my

subconscious is a mixture of all of them called Ideal LifeVision. Here's how it works. You write down in detail what you really want to have happen in several areas of your life over the next year. It is written in such a way that it creates an image in your mind, almost like a movie reel, that tells your subconscious that this is your goal and gives it clear instructions on what that goal is to look and feel like. Then you record it and listen to it over and over again as you visualize your goals being achieved. As you do this, your brain travels the path that was created by your neurons and you create a neural pathway until your subconscious has a very clear vision of what it is supposed to help you achieve and gets to work making it happen. Not only is this a great way to achieve physical goals, but I love to use it for changing thought patterns.

I have used this tool to sell a business, sell a home, start two new businesses, release weight, make and override habits, take greater responsibility, change my perspective, strengthen relationships, increase my spirituality, and learn to love myself and others on a greater level. You can find more information about the Ideal LifeVision program at www.jimmyandshelly.com/ideallifevision

I love the "Ziglar Show" podcast that features clips from Zig Ziglar's speeches and commentary from his son Tom. I was listening to episode 337 (http://zigziglar.libsyn.com/) when Tom gave the listeners a challenge: For ten days replace 15 minutes of screen time with purposeful dream time. Focus on what you want to be, do or have. He believed that doing this would bring greater clarity than most have ever experienced. His challenge resonated with me and immediately an idea came to create a resource to help myself and others gain clarity about our desires and dreams. Through a series of questions, the Dream Guide takes you through each area of your life and helps you determine where you are right now and what you want your reality to be. You can download it at www.jimmyandshelly.com.

GUT CHECK

How is your self-talk? Negative or Positive? What do you really want to believe, feel, and think? Write those things out as affirmations or use the Dream Guide to help you determine what you really want. Spend time everyday putting positive thoughts, images, and messages into your mind. And get out the backhoe if needed!

KEY # 4:

CREATE HABITS

"We are what we repeatedly do. Excellence, therefore, is not an act, but a habit."
Aristotle

Your life is the sum of your habits. If those habits are positive you tend to have positive results and are more likely to love your life. If those habits are negative, then your activities tend to lead you down a negative path, thus bringing negative results, and you are generally unhappy. How were these habits created?

HOW HABITS ARE FORMED

Imagine that you live on a deserted island. You choose to build your home up the mountain in the trees for protection. Every day you have to travel down to the water's edge to fish and wash your clothes. For the first several days you pay close attention to where your path leads and you make sure you know exactly where you are going. You pay attention to the different trees, rocks, and landmarks you pass to make sure you are on the right path. Eventually, after traveling this path multiple times, you get to the point that you don't even consciously think about how to get to the water's edge—you just find yourself there every morning.

This is how a habit is formed. It starts with a conscious thought of how to do something: How do you get to the water? What are all the steps that you need to take to get down to the water's edge? First you take one step, then another, then another. You walk around the tree, duck under the low hanging branch, then step over the creek. Once you have done this enough times, your subconscious figures out that this is a pattern it should remember, and it takes over for you so you no longer have to think about the steps to get to the water.

It's your brain's job to become as efficient as possible. Once your conscious mind has turned a task over to the subconscious, your conscious mind rarely thinks about it again. It just lets the subconscious control the action because that's one of its primary functions.

You don't think about tying your shoes, writing your name, breathing, eating, taking a drink, or even backing out of the driveway anymore. These things just happen! Research has shown that 40% of your daily activities occur this way, without any conscious decision on your part. These activities are all habitual.

This is great news if the habits you have in place are positive. If this were not so you would be so overwhelmed by your everyday actions and choices that you would be too paralyzed to do anything. Think about it. If you had to consciously tell your brain every step involved in walking every time you took off down the hall, you would never have time for anything else.

It is much like children learning to walk. When they are first getting on their feet, they struggle to focus just on getting one foot moving in front of the other. As they get more secure and their brain can handle the process a little better, they are able to move faster, perhaps even carry a toy with them. Eventually, they are running all around the house drinking from a sippy cup in one hand, with a toy in the other, and a blanket around their shoulders.

What if your habits are negative? How can you change those

habits to support you as you strive to succeed? By choosing something different.

Remember that your subconscious prides itself on its efficiency so it doesn't like it when you try to mess it up by doing something different from what it has determined to be THE way. This is one reason breaking habits can be so challenging. Your own brain doesn't want you to change what it has already determined to be sufficient. Research has shown that old neural pathways never go away — they just get overridden. How do we do that? By creating a new neural pathway or habit stronger than the old one.

Charles Duhigg's book, The Power of Habit, contains information that helps us understand how habits are made and overridden. He explains that there are three important pieces to a habit.[1]

First, you need to understand that all habits are stimulated by some kind of cue. If you have a habit of overeating, there is some kind of trigger or cue associated with it. Do you eat when you are bored, or stressed, or worried? Maybe you are triggered when you sit down to watch a movie and don't have your hands busy. Or maybe you go to the kitchen every time you feel overwhelmed. These are all cues that trigger the habit.

The second piece to a habit is the action itself. In this case, the action is the actual eating. It has become a habit for you to check the treat cupboard every time you walk in the kitchen and find something to nibble on. Once the movie goes on, do you go for the chips or ice cream?

The third piece of a habit is the reward. Once you have received a pleasurable outcome in your behavior, your brain tells you to do it again and again, eventually taking over so it can experience that reward as much as possible. You would think that your increasing waistline, the yucky feeling in your stomach when you eat sugar, and your decrease in energy wouldn't be rewards, right? Well, you are right, they're not. That is not the kind of reward my brain is looking for.

1   Charles Duhigg, The Power of Habit (New York: Random House, 2012), pw

When you eat because you are bored, your reward is a temporary focus on DOING something. You are no longer bored, even if just for a brief moment. If you eat when you are stressed, for just a few moments, you get the payoff of satisfying yourself with some form of food. In a small way, it alleviates that feeling of stress, even if just for a moment.

These are small, almost unrecognizable clues to what is driving your habit. If you don't know what the reward is, then you will struggle in trying to replace the habit, because your brain still craves that reward.

CREATING NEW AND OVERRIDING THE OLD

Think for a moment about a habit you want to change. Do you know what your trigger is? Do you know what cues lead you to that behavior? Once you have determined the cues and the behavior, look closely to determine the reward. What reward are you actually getting that makes you do this over and over again? What feeling is your brain craving that is fulfilled by your actions? Once you know the pieces of your habit, you can change it.

One way to change a habit is to find a different action that gives the same reward. What if every time you felt bored you chose to go for a walk, or read from a book? Or when you go to watch a movie, maybe you can crochet or scrapbook, or something else that helps you feel you are accomplishing something.

When you feel stressed or overwhelmed and your body craves that small rush that comes from the sugar, maybe you can go for a quick run and let the endorphins create the rush.

What if you want to create a new habit? You still need a cue, action, and reward.

A few years ago I wanted to make drinking water an integral part of my life so I decided that every time I passed a drinking fountain I was going to stop and take a drink, whether I was thirsty or not.

My cue was seeing the drinking fountain. The action was taking the drink. The reward was the knowledge that I was giving my body what it needed and that I was fulfilling a goal I had. Now, a few years later, I don't even think about taking a drink. I just automatically bend down and gulp anytime I see a drinking fountain. It has become a habit that is turned over to my subconscious. This may seem really basic and simple, but it works.

When I was in high school I got really sick of having bad days and decided that there were only good days. I wanted viewing my days as good to become a habit. My trigger was being asked how my day was. It happened almost daily, so I was consistently triggered. Then, for the first few months, I made the conscious decision to say "I am having a good day," whether I believed it or not. The reward was that slight and small peaceful feeling I got from knowing that I was choosing to see things differently. After a few months, I no longer had to choose to say it — it just came out. And that is when I realized that I was truly thinking differently and had created a new habit that overrode the old one.

YOU MUST BELIEVE

Duhigg affirms there is one essential key to creating lasting habits or overriding old ones. You must believe in your heart that it is possible to change! If you don't, you can achieve temporary results, but when things get hard, you will resort back to what worked every other time. When you believe, and have others who believe in you and have shown you it can be done, then you are more likely to stick to it and trust the process.[2]

Do you have a support system? Do you have people who love you and want your success and have also done it themselves? It is important to find mentors and friends who will continually pull you along, stand by your side, or even gently nudge you from behind when necessary. I know first-hand how important it is to have someone who understands where you've been and also knows where you are going. But not all support is created equal.

2   Ibid.

Make sure that you have someone who really understands your goals and can and will support you free of judgment and with your best interest at heart.

HABITUAL THINKING

I read a statistic recently that stated that 95% of all our thoughts are the same thoughts we had yesterday, and the day before, and the day before that. That means those thoughts are habitual. The statistic then stated that 80% of those thoughts are negative. Those are pretty depressing numbers. But I believe them.

IS BEING A VICTIM A HABIT?

Have you ever wondered if victimhood is a habit? Or maybe excuses and blaming have become second nature to you. You are triggered by a situation, an opportunity to shift the blame. Your action is the excuse — telling the victim story — and the reward is the attention you get from it. Many thrive on the feeling of martyrdom, victimhood, or sacrifice. And they love it when people acknowledge them for it and build them up because of it. It is a pretty significant reward.

I had a client once tell me her daughter was concerned with how much she exaggerates things. She is a really great storyteller but when she tells a story, it does not always contain the true details of what happened. It seems that the fish is always two feet longer than it really was, or the event is way more dramatic than what occurred. For a while she got a lot of attention for her stories. Kids would be asking for more and more details and hanging on every word. She received a rush from the attention. Exaggerating became a habit. But now she is realizing that the kids don't believe her anymore, and the reward is fading. She now wants to change the habit into truth telling. The trigger is the same: an event will occur and she will want to tell you about it. The action is telling the truth. And the reward is the attention she gets because we can trust what she is saying.

KEYSTONE HABITS

Let me share one last idea from The Power of Habit: "The habits that matter most are the ones that, when they start to shift, dislodge and remake other patterns." These are called keystone habits. Often, just creating a positive habit in your life will eliminate many of the negative habits.[3]

I have found that for me and many of my clients, one of the most powerful keystone habits is exercise. When you are exercising regularly, it has so many positive effects on your brain that your need for some of your other negative habits (like sugar, overeating, and apathy) disappear. Finding your keystone habits will eliminate a lot of wasted time trying to conquer other habits that will naturally go away.

GUT CHECK

What habits are you wanting to change or override? What habits do you want to develop? If it is something new, build in a trigger—something you do every day without fail that you can rely on to be a cue. Determine the action you want to participate in, and figure out what reward will drive you. What keystone habits could you start implementing?

3   Ibid.

KEY # 5:

DEVELOP GRATITUDE

"Gratitude is not only the greatest of virtues, but the parent of all others."
Cicero

For many years I have heard the divine principle of gratitude and thanksgiving be preached. I have been reminded frequently of the scripture that says

"Thou shalt thank the Lord thy God in all things....

And in nothing doth man offend God, or against none is his wrath kindled, save those who confess not his hand in all things."[1]

It was not until recently that I have gained a truer understanding of why gratitude is so important in our lives and the profound effect it can have on our mindset.

A few months ago I saw a movie called The Letter Writer in which actor Bernie Diamond portrays an aged gentleman in a care center. Every day Bernie's character Sam picks a random name and address from the phone book and writes an uplifting letter to the lucky recipient.

---

1   Doctrine & Covenants 59:7,21

Part way through the touching movie, Sam and Maggie, a young teenage girl who received one of his letters, spend the day giving away handwritten note cards to strangers throughout the town. The result was very touching, and an idea was sparked in my own mind.

What if I wrote one note card every day for 30 days to anyone whom I felt impressed to thank? I can tell you that the results from my "experiment" changed my perspective on the world. Every day I found myself looking for the good that others were doing. I was constantly looking to find those unsung heroes, like the school bus driver, the church teacher, and the kind neighbor whose service often went unnoticed. I thought of old friends, acquaintances, and people who had influenced my life to whom I could spread some sunshine.

You can guess what happened. My whole attitude toward the world around me and the people in it changed. I noticed the good that was ever abundant in an increasingly wicked world. I witnessed circumstances in which people had every reason to complain, yet chose to have a cheerful attitude, and I became grateful for my own struggles. I was overwhelmed by the love I felt for complete strangers whose story I never learned, but who needed a kind word.

Thomas S. Monson has said that "Sincerely giving thanks not only helps us recognize our blessings, but it also unlocks the doors of heaven and helps us feel God's love."[2] I know that is what happened for me during my experiment. And who doesn't want to feel more of God's love?

GRATITUDE LIST

I was taught another tool of gratitude by a dear friend and mentor Dr. Paul Jenkins.

I was struggling to feel grateful for a specific aspect of my life.

2   Thomas S. Monson, "The Divine Gift of Gratitude," Ensign, Nov 2010.

It was something I wanted to change right away but didn't have the power to control at the moment. The overwhelming thoughts of how bad I wanted something different were starting to affect my own happiness and permeate my thoughts. Dr. Paul invited me to try a little challenge.

For seven days I was to make a list of at least 12 reasons I appreciated this specific part of my life. After just a few days, I felt a major shift in my thinking and my gratitude for what I did have increased while my discontent and discouragement diminished.

I now invite all my clients and you to do a similar exercise every day. Many of my students have claimed that this is the single most important thing they do every day to win the mind game. When they find themselves struggling with a circumstance, they immediately find five reasons they are grateful for it.

GRATITUDE PULLS US OUT OF THE FUNK

One of the most powerful things about gratitude is that is helps pull you out of what I call "The Funk." During those times when you are low and feeling discouraged or down, just taking a few minutes to think about the things you are grateful for can instantly change your mood.

I have loved hearing different ways the Gratitude List has been used. One mother shared that when she was frustrated with her children and was ready to explode, she took a quick time out and listed five reasons she was grateful for them. Almost instantly, she was on a different thought path and could assess the situation with a clear mind and a loving heart.

One woman told me that she stopped her husband in the middle of an argument and started listing reasons she was grateful for him. Again, almost instantly, the hostility changed to appreciation and they were able to talk over their situation with love and kindness.

Gordon B. Hinckley said, "When you walk with gratitude, you

do not walk with arrogance and conceit and egotism, you walk with a spirit of thanksgiving that is becoming to you and will bless your lives."[3]

EVALUATION OR CREATION

Do you struggle with the idea that the grass is greener on the other side? If you're constantly evaluating your reality against something that appears to be better it will bring discouragement and disappointment. If you would instead look at "what is" and compare it with all the things that could be so much worse, you would find yourself full of gratitude for what you already have.

It is common to get caught in the "I'll be happy when…" syndrome. Or the "If only…."

"If only we had more money to do x, y, and z. Then we would be happy."

"I'll be happy when the business is all set up and making money."

"Life would be so much better if we had a bigger house."

Take a moment to gain true gratitude for "what is". Only then can you step out of evaluation mode into creation mode and have the ability to create something better. It is possible to be content with where and who you are, and at the same time not be content to stay there permanently.[4]

The truth is maybe the people living on the other side are already in creation mode! They have put in the work to fertilize, water, weed, mow, and edge their grass. Beautifully manicured lawns don't just grow perfectly on their own. You must take responsibility and do the work to become who you want to become, and the rest will follow. Trust me!

---

3   Gordon B. Hinckley, Teachings of Gordon B. Hinckley (1997), 250

4   Paul Jenkins PhD, Pocket Positivity (Orem UT 2015)

HALF-TIME PEP TALK

Let's have a Pep Talk.

By now you are realizing that this work of Mastering Your Mindset takes a lot of effort and diligence. It's like my friend and mentor Dr. Paul Jenkins says: "Elevation takes effort!" If you are going to make a difference you are going to have to work for it.

But the fact that you haven't closed the cover of this book and given up altogether shows you are serious about changing your life. I want to thank you for putting the time and work into making these shifts happen in your own life. Continue to be diligent in your efforts and the payoff will come — sometimes without you even realizing it.

A few years ago my husband and I were struggling to build our printing business and were implementing some major changes. One of the changes meant letting go of employees who had been part of our team for several years. It was a challenging time, filled with many prayers, tears, and heartache. As rough as that experience was, a small miracle occurred partway through. In the midst of the turmoil, I realized that not only was I not overcome with fear and doubt (which I expected), but I was actually grateful for the things the Lord was teaching us during that time. He was giving us the answers step by step, line upon line. They were lessons that we needed to learn not just for that specific moment, but for many other moments later. It was at that time that I realized that my mindset really had changed. I was seeing and thinking about things differently. It felt subtle, almost unrecognizable, except that at that moment I didn't feel like the world was crashing in on me. And I was able to have gratitude IN THE MOMENT of the trial instead of several years down the road. It was a huge breakthrough for me!

Those moments will come for you, too! At some point you are going to go through something and notice that you are thinking about it differently. You are going to notice that your perception or perspective of things has changed and you didn't even realize it. You are going to notice that your faith and trust has increased and your ability to be grateful and happy has grown in ways you never recognized. If you continue to do the work (and there will always be work to do), the results will come. I promise!

KEY # 6:

BUILD YOUR CONFIDENCE

"Not feeling good about yourself can be a very selfish pastime."
Doug Nielsen, Take Life by the Helm

I have heard from so many women (and men) that one of the things that keeps them from being the person they want to be is a lack of confidence. Though it is part of my nature to be a performer and I have been both socially and competitively for almost 32 years, I have personally struggled with confidence most of my life. Someone who loves being in front of a large audience isn't confident? How can that be?

WHAT IS TRUE CONFIDENCE?

I used to believe, as do many people in the world, that confidence was the ability to get up in front of people, to be able to talk to people without hesitation, to be able to perform, or to sell something with ease. Because that was my definition, I viewed people who did that as confident, and people who didn't as lacking. I was doing those things and outwardly looked and seemed confident. But inside I was not.

I believe you can do those things whether you are confident or not. But I also believe that doing those things well is a byproduct of being confident.

True confidence is knowing who you are and not needing anyone else's approval. It is not "I hope people like me," but rather, "I will be ok if they don't." True confidence comes from within and doesn't require external praise or personal boasting. It doesn't have room for jealousy or envy. A confident person can be aware of someone else's accomplishments, gifts, or beauty without comparing it to their own.

Confidence is not something most people are born with—it's a choice and a habit. Just as perfecting a piano piece takes work and practice, so does building your confidence.

Building your confidence is like building a muscle; the more you use it, the stronger it gets. So, what are the steps to building that confidence muscle or habit?

MAKE A DECISION

First, start with making the conscious choice that you want to be confident. I know this sounds like a no-brainer, but until you have set the intention to build your confidence, and you are fully committed to doing so, you will go nowhere. Decide in your own mind what a confident you looks like. Can you see it as if you were watching a movie of yourself? Imagine yourself navigating sticky situations with courage. Picture yourself having conversations, giving presentations, working through problems, or dealing with criticism or negativity. Imagine situations you have been in before when you wished you had dealt with them differently. What does differently look like? How does the "ideal" you behave and feel as you experience these things confidently? Once you have created a great visual for yourself, replay it over and over again in your mind, several times a day, for multiple days. Plant the vision within your subconscious of what you want yourself to be. Create the self-image around that person.

KNOW WHO YOU REALLY ARE

Confidence is gained from knowing who you truly are. Too often we think it's who we are that is keeping us from the life of our dreams. But truly, the real problem lies in who we think we aren't. As Zig Ziglar states, "Most people have a picture of themselves that is so narrow and so shallow it bears no resemblance to who they are and what they can do. Most people have no idea what they can do, because all they've been told is what they can NOT do. Most people don't know what they can do because they don't know who they are."[1]

Do you know who you really are? Do you like who you really are? Have you spent time with yourself discovering what makes you tick, what motivates you, what gets you excited? Do you know what your strengths and weaknesses are?

Many people in the world struggle to answer yes to those questions. If you are one of them you may feel trapped living a life that you think everyone else wants you to live and that can really affect your confidence.

Take some time to ponder and write about the answers to the following questions. They may start to give you insight into who you really are.

1. What makes you genuinely happy?

2. When do you feel most connected to yourself and God?

3. What would you do if you knew you could not fail?

4. What lights you up—gets you excited?

5. What are your core personal values?

6. What would you do with your day if money wasn't an issue?

---

1   Ziglar, podcast

7. What are your strengths? Passions? Talents? (What is easy and effortless for you to do?)

8. Do you enjoy spending time alone, or with company?

9. Do you find solutions to problems as you talk it out with other people, or as you think within yourself?

Some of these questions may seem hard to answer for yourself and you may need a friend or family member you trust to give you some insight.

A few years ago I was not sure if I could answers those questions for myself. I was faking happiness and trying to appear that I loved my life. Yet I had laid aside many of my greatest gifts and joys or mislabeled them as weaknesses. It wasn't until I came across the "Uniquely Me" training by professional profiler and style expert Krista Nebeker (www.kristanebeker.com) that my perception of myself started to change.

This training helped me start to understand and love my true self, the person God had created me to be. I started to realize that I had spent my life hiding my true strengths, believing they were actually weaknesses, and focusing on all the things I didn't think I was capable of doing. When I learned what those true gifts and talents were, I quit beating myself up over what I wasn't and started celebrating what I was.

This process of growth has taken years and still continues today. It is not something that can be shared in a paragraph, or even a chapter of a book. It is an entire book itself (which I hope to write someday). It starts with letting go of all the guilt and shame of who you thought you were supposed to be, and focusing instead on who you really are: a person with unique power given to you by a loving Creator. You are a person with special gifts, talents, challenges, and weaknesses that help you grow and bless God's other children. Your individual perspectives and life experiences, paired with your distinct talents and strengths, are your gifts to others in this life. When you use these gifts the way God intended you will find great satisfaction and joy (and confidence)!

Don't be a second rate version of someone else when you can be a first rate version of yourself.

LIVE TRUE TO YOUR CORE

When you are not living up to the core values you have determined for yourself, your confidence will be lacking. If I asked you today what your core values are, could you answer? Maybe you could put your finger on one or two, maybe a few more. Many of us haven't spent much time thinking about what is really important to us. A few years ago I had the opportunity to revisit these core values at a business retreat. The exercise went something like this.

"You are sent to another planet to start your own world. You are allowed to have 5 values present on this planet. Which would you choose?" Here are a few to get your wheels turning.

FAMILY	HONESTY	FREEDOM	COOPERATION
LOYALTY	INDEPENDENCE	HARD WORK	RESOURCEFUL-NESS
SELF-RELIANCE	FAIRNESS	DIVERSITY	CREATIVITY
SPIRITUALITY	CHANGE	ORDER	OBEDIENCE
OPTIMISM	GRATITUDE	TEAM WORK	PURPOSE
LOVE	WEALTH	ACCOMPLISH-MENT	TRUTH

If you are not living a core-centered life, you are probably living a "default" life instead. If you have forgotten, ignored, or minimized what you believe deep inside, you may find yourself being bent by whatever the world around you determines important.

When you live this kind of life, you find that you aren't truly happy. You have a dissonance within in your soul that can only be resolved by living true to those beliefs.

CHALLENGE YOURSELF

One of the quickest ways to build self-confidence is to do exactly what you are afraid to do.

Why? Because facing your fears gives you strength and courage. And knowing that you can face things that scare you will automatically having you walking taller and believing in yourself more.

QUIT COMPARING

True confidence comes from within and is something no one can give you or take away from you. But there are often times when other factors will greatly diminish your ability to see yourself clearly, as a son or daughter of God who has a divine role and purpose here on this earth.

Zig Ziglar said this: "You were designed for accomplishment, engineered for success, and endowed with the seeds of greatness."[2] All this came from a loving Creator who wants you to believe in yourself and your abilities as much as He believes in you.

There is something that gets in the way of us seeing that greatness more than almost anything. It is the destructive habit of comparing ourselves with others. This gets us in trouble in multiple ways.

First, we often compare someone's highlight reel with our behind-the-scenes.

We see someone's outward display, and compare it with what we have going on in our head. We don't see the turmoil they

2   Ibid.

may be going through, the heartache or grinding work they are putting in to get where they are. We just assume they fell there. Well, people at the top of the mountain don't just fall there. But that may be all we see, them standing on the top of the mountain, while we gruelingly trudge our way through the brush, weeds, and rocks to reach the top. Then we assume we don't measure up to them because we are not where they are. Well, have we done the work yet to get there? Maybe not.

Second, we worry about how others might see us.

For example, have you ever gone to church and seen the mom who seems to have it all together? Her kids are sitting perfectly in pressed dresses with shined shoes and their hair is beautifully done. You walk in late and look down at your kids who have wet hair, crumpled clothes because you pulled them out of the laundry basket (that's been sitting there for the last week!), and throw-up stains on your baby because they puked as you walked out the door and you didn't take time to change them. You compare yourself to that other mom, secretly envious that she is so amazing, and you wonder why you are such a failure. And if that is not enough, you assume that everyone else is thinking the same thing. Well, stop it! Only you can control the comparing. No one else can wave their magic wand and make you stop judging yourself against everyone else.

On those days when you really do feel like a failure and your confidence is lower than it's ever been, remember that some of the greatest successes in the world were told they were failures. But they rose in spite of the criticism and comparing. And you can, too!

Think of Oprah Winfrey, who was demoted from her job as a news anchor because she "wasn't fit for television." Or Walt Disney, who was fired from a newspaper for "lacking imagination" and "having no original ideas." What about The Beatles, who were told they had "no future in show business." And even Albert Einstein was told he would "never amount to much."

More often than not we determine our confidence by how we think others see us, or by what they tell us. When our happiness and confidence level are dependent on someone else, we give away some of our agency to others.

Remember my friend who wanted her mom to say the right things so she could feel loved and confident? Her internal happiness and confidence was always dependent on her mom. But she couldn't control her mom or her actions, so my friend always felt defeated, until she finally realized that confidence comes from within. And although it makes all of us feel good to have others believe in us, and it does help temporarily, it is fleeting and won't last. Only confidence that comes from knowing deep within who we are and not needing others' approval can sustain us throughout the intense ups and downs of this mortal existence.

If you live off a man's compliments, you'll die from his criticism.

TAKE CARE OF YOURSELF

There are times our confidence can be altered by physical things like sleep, exercise, and eating properly. Sometimes even a simple shower can help raise your energy level and help you take the day head on.

Take care of yourself. I am not talking about being selfish and greedy and needing a break. I am talking about making sure your body has the fuel it needs to do all that is required of it. I have learned for myself that my natural energy is very high and requires a lot of sleep and food to maintain. If I am not taking care of myself physically, my confidence will plummet simply because I don't have the energy to maintain it.

COMMIT TO DAILY ESSENTIALS

Commit to some kind of daily essentials. These are things you do every day to connect to God and your own spirit; things that inspire and motivate you.

When I start my day off with these essential things, and continue them throughout the day, I find I have more confidence and strength to do what I need to do. I am connected to God and am listening for what He wants me to do. I feel His love and that breeds true confidence, a confidence that comes from knowing I am right with God and not needing anyone else's approval. This is a confidence that doesn't look side to side, but up and within for approval.[3]

I am talking about taking a minute to connect with God and yourself so that you can feel who you really are. It is a matter of making sure your spiritual, emotional and physical buckets are full so that there is plenty to share with others. You want to be spilling over to others all the time. And confidence can come from knowing you have something to share.

CONTROL YOUR THOUGHTS

Learn how to talk to yourself. We have already discussed in Chapter 3 the self-talk cycle. Learn to stop the negative chatter in your head that seeks to destroy your confidence. Spend time daily repeating personal affirmations and filling your mind and heart with positive and confident thoughts. What you think about grows, so choose your thoughts wisely.

And by all means, quit telling yourself how you wish you were confident. You get what you think about so align your thoughts on what you want to be, not what you aren't! Be aware of each time your thoughts go down the toxic path. Redirect them by consciously choosing to think the opposite.

BE HUMBLE

Truly confident individuals are humble. What does it take to

3   Shelly Coray. RISE UP Daily Essentials (2015). (www. jimmyandshelly.com/rise-up-daily-essentials)

be humble, to let go of our pride? First let us define pride. Pride is putting our will against God or our fellowmen and is competitive in nature.

In the words of C. S. Lewis: "Pride gets no pleasure out of having something, only out of having more of it than the next man.... It is the comparison that makes you proud: the pleasure of being above the rest. Once the element of competition has gone, pride has gone."[4]

Ezra Taft Benson said "When pride has a hold on our hearts, we lose our independence of the world and deliver our freedoms to the bondage of men's judgment."[5]

In other words, you give up to others around you your ability to be happy and have confidence when you are filled with pride. As stated before, are you looking from side-to- side for approval and validation instead of up and within? True humility brings a deep rooted level of confidence that no one can take from you.

LIVE INTENTIONALLY

Remember the woman a few chapters back who said that going a week without making excuses for her choices and mistakes gave her more power. She also stated that it naturally increased her confidence. Why? The power of not justifying her actions or blaming someone or something else raised her confidence and strengthened her ability to make better choices. She began to live more intentionally and make choices based on her core values. It eliminated the dissonant feeling that often erodes our confidence.

The more you love your own decisions the less you need others to love them.

The day you can choose to do something just because you want to, not because you are afraid of what others may think, is a very

4   C.S. Lewis, Mere Christianity (New York: Harper One, Oct 2012)
5   Ezra Taft Benson, "Beware of Pride," Ensign, May 1989

liberating day.

SURROUND YOURSELF WITH THINGS THAT INSPIRE YOU

It has been said that you are the sum of the five people you spend the most time with. Would you want to be the average of those people? Do they inspire you? Do they motivate you? Do you want to be your best when you are around them? Do they understand your goals and dreams and support you to follow them? Or do they exhaust you? Be very aware of energy vampires who suck the life right out of you. Your confidence can't afford to spend time with them on a regular basis.

Now think about your environment, the places you spend your time. Do they inspire you or exhaust you? Do you enjoy where you work? Does your bedroom invite you to peaceful sleep? Does your office entice and motivate you to do your best work?

Remember that you can change who you are and where you are by changing what you put into your mind. Do you have uplifting messages around your home? Are you watching, reading, and listening to media that uplifts you and motivates you, or exhaust you and brings you down?

Be very conscious and intentional about what is going into your mind and what and who you surround yourself with.

GUT CHECK

Are you comparing yourself to others? Are you living up to your core? Are you looking side to side for validation? Are you taking care of yourself physically and spiritually? Are you making poor choices and blaming or making excuses? Do you have negative thought patterns that need to be replaced? Are you grateful? Is your environment uplifting? Are you spending time with people you inspire you?

KEY # 7:

CHOOSE COURAGE

"Courage is resistance to fear, mastery of fear — not absence of fear. Except a creature be part coward, it is not a compliment to say it is brave!"
Mark Twain

When I was a freshman in high school I was a member of the school track team. Beause of my height, I ended up at the hurdles and the high jump. All through pre-season I prepared for both events with excitement and determination (and a lot of trepidation). They both required going over an obstacle that has the ability to hurt you if you don't do it right.

At the first track meet my adrenaline was pumping and my nerves were on high alert as I ran around the track for my warm-up. Both events were at the beginning of the meet. I rounded the corner of the track and looked over to where the high jump mat should have been. Instead of a 12' by 18' by 24" high mat, I saw a net filled with foam wedges that was not very far off the ground. I panicked. I was overcome with fear. My mind started racing with all the possibilities of things that could go wrong. What if I missed the wedges and ended up on the asphalt? What if I knocked the bar off and landed on it? What if I missed everything altogether and made a complete fool of myself? I couldn't handle the pressure and I never showed up for that event. In fact, although I continued to practice high jump all year long, I never competed in it at a single meet. I think it's safe to say that I didn't navigate that fear well and most certainly did not have success. Fear won!

Fear is often the single most limiting factor to our success and happiness. Fear is always going to be part of your life. The way you navigate through the fear will determine your level of success.

WHAT IS FEAR?

Back in the caveman days, a feeling of fear was an indicator of danger. When you or your family were faced with it, you would feel the physical effects of fear so that it would heighten your awareness and keep you alert. That feeling still exists today. It's called visceral fear. It's the feeling of being chased by a bear, or getting too close to the edge of the cliff, or driving too fast on the icy roads. Pay attention to these feelings. They are there for your safety!

Visceral fear is not what keeps you from success. It keeps you from doing something really stupid that could cause major harm to your body or spirit.

The fear that gets in your way is self-created. It is defined as an imagined negative outcome in the future appearing real. Remember the high jump? All I could think about was everything that could go wrong. Craig Manning writes in his book The Fearless Mind: "Fear only exists in our thoughts of what may or may not happen in the future."[1] This fear that something will or won't happen will often keep you from doing the things that will really bring great success and happiness.

A few chapters ago we talked about the functions of the subconscious mind. One of its jobs is to store every bit of information we have ever been exposed to so the conscious mind can use it later when it's trying to make a decision.

1   Craig Manning, Fearless Mind (Springville UT: Cedar Fort, Inc. 2010)

At that first track meet my conscious mind was trying to decide whether to high jump or not. It started pulling things up from my subconscious that I had experienced, witnessed, or imagined associated with high jumping; people landing on the bar, missing the pit, or just plain looking foolish. My conscious mind was evaluating, "There haven't been good experiences in the past, and the future will be the same. I don't want to feel that way." The decision was made — "No, we are not high jumping, today."

Knowing that fear is actually self-created is good news! Because you created it, you can also be the one to stop it. What would you do if you were not afraid? The truth is, your level of success is determined by how often you choose courage when faced with fear.

Before we get into the actual strategies of dealing with fear, I want to share a new perspective on fear so that you can learn to see it a little differently.

CHANGE YOUR PERSPECTIVE ON FEAR

First, fear is our body's way of signaling to us that we are not comfortable. And since we know that success and growth are just outside our comfort zone, fear can actually be a good sign. If you are experiencing great levels of fear, you can look forward to experiencing great levels of growth as well (as long as you choose to confront the fear).

Many people will do anything to avoid the uncomfortable feelings of fear. Those who do run an even bigger risk of never getting what they want. Most of the good stuff requires taking a risk and facing your fears.

Second, fear can be an indicator that something is important to you. Steven Pressfield shares in his book, The War of Art, that "... The more fear we feel about a specific enterprise, the more certain we can be that the enterprise is important to us and the growth of our soul...If it meant nothing to us, there'd be no resistance.... So if you didn't love the project that is terrifying you, you wouldn't feel anything."[2]

Jack Canfield says, "Think of fear as a 2-year-old child who doesn't want to go grocery shopping with you. You wouldn't let a 2-year-old's mentality run your life. Because you must buy groceries, you'll just have to take the 2-year-old along with you. Fear is no different. In other words, acknowledge that fear exists but don't let it keep you from doing important tasks."[3]

Also, recognize that the fear is created by an adversary that doesn't want your growth! For me that adversary is Satan. Satan doesn't want you to find joy and happiness and especially not success. He doesn't want you to bless others. He wants you to fail. He is going to use any tactic he can to get you to stop and retreat. The seed of fear is planted by the Devil. It's your choice whether to let it grow or not. How long are you going to sit by and let him run your life? Use the energy is takes to be fearful and full of worry and use it to fight the real adversary.

On the same note, I love this visual from Dieter F. Uchtdorf. He states: "[God] is constantly raining blessings down on us [blessings of courage, of strength, of success]. It is our own doubt, fear, and sin that, like an umbrella, block these blessings from reaching us."[4]

If you really want to take down that umbrella and be open to all that God has to offer you, you must overcome the doubt and fear and not let Satan win.

So how do we do that?

OVERCOMING FEAR

First, choose courage. I asked a group of 11-year-olds what courage was. They said things like:

---

2   Steven Pressfield, The War of Art (New York, Black Irish Entertainment LLC, 2002)
3   Canfield, op. cit.
4   Uchtdorf, "Live the Gospel Joyful" Church News, 28 Sept 2014

"You aren't afraid."

"You are brave."

"Stuff doesn't scare you."

I have to admit, until a few years ago I thought the same things,- so I didn't consider myself a very courageous person. It wasn't until I remembered a quote by John Wayne in the movie True Grit: "Courage is being scared to death and saddling up anyway." that my perspective changed. I realized that courage is not the absence of fear. Courage is feeling the fear, and doing what must be done anyway. So when you are faced with something that scares you, your first step is to put on your courage armor and face the fight!

I recently took my family to a local swimming pool and I had no idea the fear challenge that would come from it. I have a love/hate relationship with fear challenges. I hate doing things that are scary and hard for me, but I love putting on my courage armor and building my confidence.

It started with my seven-year-old wanting to learn how to swim. She was struggling to even get her face under the water. So I offered her ice cream. Some of you call it a bribe; I call it motivation. Whatever you call it, it worked! And soon all three of my daughters were wondering how they could earn ice cream, too.

My five-year-old looked longingly at the kiddie slide in the splash pad area. I asked her if she wanted to go down it, and she nodded. But she said she was too scared. I knew I could figure out how to get her down this slide if I used my "fear tactics." So I started with motivation.

"Honey, I will give you an ice cream cone if you go down the slide." The right motivation is sometimes enough, but not for her. Next, I started to determine where the real fear was coming from. I asked, "What part of going down the slide are you afraid of?"

It turns out that she was afraid of the water splashing up in her face when she reached the bottom of the slide. So we watched many others and realized that the person who designed this slide was a genius. No matter the size of the child, the water never splashed above the neck. First obstacle - overcome!

She was also afraid of a large bucket that dumped water on the person at the top of the slide. We counted the seconds it took for the bucket to fill up before dumping and determined she would have 13 seconds to get to the top of the slide and go down before the bucket would dump again. Second obstacle - check!

During this process of overcoming obstacles, we heard a blood-curdling scream. We watched as a mother did the straight jacket hold on her son and forced him down the slide on her lap, hoping he would jump up at the bottom and say "That was so fun mommy, let's do it again." Nope. Now he was even more terrified, and he didn't trust the person who was supposed to protect him.

As my little one inched her way closer to the stairs I told her I would hold her hand as she came down the slide. When she got to the bottom, she looked back at me grinning from ear to ear, asking to go down again! Our fear of something is usually worse than the thing itself. If we could just find the courage to do what we need to do we would find that it isn't as bad as we think!

Throughout the course of the evening all my daughters not only went on the adult slides with Daddy, but eventually went on the big kid slides all by themselves. In fact, we had to drag them off to go home.

All of my children had completed an extreme fear challenge that night and had earned not just one scoop of ice cream, but three. They were not the only ones who faced a fear challenge that night...

They kept asking me what I was going to do to earn my ice cream. I would have been pretty happy to skip out on the treat, but then I looked down and saw who was watching.

I knew I had to face the only thing in the pool that scared me, a 12-foot cliff. There was no working my way up to it – there wasn't anything in the pool that was smaller. This was one of those moments when I just had to jump. I climbed the stairs and walked to the edge of the cliff where I almost lost everything I had eaten in the last week. I stepped back off the ledge, willing myself to have the courage to jump. I took a deep breath and stepped up to the ledge again, looking to the side of the pool where my family was waiting. I exhaled, then backed up again and started towards the stairs feeling defeated. All at once my kids started yelling, "Mom, jump, in 3, 2..." and the whole pool joined in for "1!". I turned back towards the ledge and ran for it. When I surfaced and saw the look on my children's face I couldn't help but feel more confident. I had shown them that I could do hard things, and they had shown me the same.

Once you have chosen courage and experienced overcoming fear for yourself, it is much easier to do it over and over again. It gives you strength! But you have to take the first step.

There are many different ways to deal with fear. But here are a few things we can learn from that experience:

1. Find your motivation. What will get you going and keep you going when things get rough?

2. Uncover the real fears. Once you discover what the real fear is, you can often find a work-around or eliminate the fear all together. Here's a little exercise I learned from Jack Canfield: List one thing you are really afraid of doing (like picking up a spider, climbing a ladder, making a sales call, etc.) Now write this out: "I really want to _____ but I scare myself by imagining_____."

3. Take it a step at a time and work up to it if you can. Start with the kiddie slide.

4. Get support. Find someone who has been there and can hold your hand.

5. Jump if you have to.

6. Remember a time when you chose courage and take yourself back there.

7. Focus on what you want to feel instead. Your mind can't deal with both emotions at the same time.

8. Determine the worst-case scenario and how you would deal with it. Sometimes just knowing you have a plan eliminates the fear all together.

9. Realize it's a two-year-old or an adversary trying to get you to buckle and run away. Put on your courage armor and face the fight.

10. Engage in a gratitude list. What are five reasons you will be grateful you faced your fear?

FEAR OF SUCCESS

I often hear from clients that they are actually afraid of success. It used to make me scratch my head. Some are afraid of the lifestyle change that would come with success; some are afraid of the attention. But I believe that the real fear of success stems from the fear of letting our light shine. I love how Marianne Williamson put it:

> Our deepest fear is not that we are inadequate. Our deepest fear is that we are powerful beyond measure. It is our light, not our darkness that most frightens us. We ask ourselves, who am I to be brilliant, gorgeous, talented, fabulous? Actually, who are you not to be? You are a child of God. Your playing small does not serve the world. There is nothing enlightened about shrinking so that other people won't feel insecure around you. We are all meant to shine, as children do. We were born to

make manifest the glory of God that is within us. It's not just in some of us; it's in everyone. And as we let our own light shine, we unconsciously give other people permission to do the same. As we are liberated from our own fear, our presence automatically liberates others.[5]

GUT CHECK

What are you really afraid of? In what ways can you put on your courage armor and face the fight? Are you hiding your light? What ways can you start small and build your courage muscles? How is fear holding you back from truly becoming the person you we created to be?

5   Marianne Williamson, A Return to Love: Reflections on the Principles of "A Course in Miracles" (New York: Harper One, 1996)

KEY # 8:

CHANGE YOUR PERSPECTIVE

*"We can complain because rose bushes have thorns, or
rejoice because thorn bushes have roses."*
Abraham Lincoln

WHAT'S YOUR PERSPECTIVE?

Stephen R. Covey said, "We see the world, not as it is, but as we are, or as we are conditioned to see it." This is called perspective. The dictionary defines "perspective" as "a particular attitude toward or way of regarding something; a point of view." It is the lens through which we see life. Our point of view can come from many places — our parents, our experiences, our trials and challenges, or things we pick up from the world. And often we assume that what we think is true. But don't believe everything you think. Sometimes how we are seeing things isn't really a true representation of the situation at all.

You have probably heard that you can change your life by changing the stories you tell yourself. To change those stories we often need a change of perspective. That change in perspective will give us the ability to start doing things differently.

Doing things differently starts with seeing things differently.

And seeing things differently starts with thinking about things differently. You must be aware that your paradigms or thought patterns need to change if anything in your life is going to change.

ARE YOUR CIRCUMSTANCES A BLESSING?

Some time ago I had the opportunity to be taught by an amazing fellow speaker, Chad Hymas. One hour of learning from Chad changed my life forever.

Several years ago, Chad was living the life of his dreams. He was married, with a darling little boy, running a very successful landscaping business, and building an elk ranch, which had been a lifelong dream. He got a call one night that his little boy had taken his first steps. He rushed home to see the action, stopping to feed the elk before going up to the house. In his haste, he loaded the forklift, which was low on hydraulic fluid, with a one-ton bale of hay. The hydraulic fluid failed and the bale of hay fell on top of Chad's neck, pinning him in the forklift.

Chad was eventually rescued but had lost all use of his limbs from the neck down. He was now a quadriplegic. For weeks, Chad felt sorry for himself. That all changed when Chad was invited to tell his story to a church congregation. Someone in the audience was touched by his story and asked Chad if he would speak to his company about his experience. He offered to pay him a few thousand dollars. Thus started Chad's speaking career. Today, Chad speaks all over the world and is known in the speaking industry as one of the most influential speakers alive.

Chad's perspective on his accident helped me to gain a new perspective on the challenges I have faced and will face in the future.

His wife quoted in his book, Doing What Must Be Done:

"What seemed a tragedy has redefined itself as a gift. Actually, it didn't redefine itself. Chad's attitude and approach have redefined it."[1]

It was Chad's response to the event and circumstance that changed his outcome. And the perspective he gained changed not only his life, but thousands upon thousands of others who have heard him speak.

We know that our attitude determines our altitude. So I want to ask you this question: When things get tough and life throws you a curve ball, what is your attitude? What is your perspective?

HELL IS ESSENTIAL TO HEALING

One particular treatment during Chad's long recover was especially challenging. He described it as a fire hydrant flooding his lungs and drowning him. Every time it happened he thought he was going to die. In his book he said "The procedure lasts less than a minute, but it is pure Hell." And then he followed with, "Hell is sometimes essential to healing."[2]

Wow! What an attitude to have. Had they not flushed his lungs he would not have survived.

So what hell are you going through, or have been through? Did you see it as something that helped you heal and grow, or as something to tear you down? Sometimes when we are in the moment and things are dark, it is challenging for us to see the good. It is at those times that we must ask ourselves how we are going to use the experiences given to us in this mortal life.

Do you see life as hard? That word leaves a bad taste in my mouth and gives my perspective or my attitude a negative spin. But a challenge—now that's something I can get excited about. A challenge is an adventure, something I can conquer. And conquer I will! And so can you!

Chad had every reason in the world to give up and become a victim. Instead he said "Don't give in to your deprivations.

1   Chad Hymas, Doing What Must Be Done (Chad Hymas, 2011)
2   Ibid.

Live up to your expectations….Spending too much time in regret denies us the opportunity of getting the most out of our experience-devastating though the experience may seem."[3]

I have had the opportunity to spend time with many people who have overcome great obstacles. There is one thing they all have in common; they believed that their challenge could and would make them stronger. They refused to be the victim, but took responsibility in the situation, regardless of whose "fault" is might have been. They took action and didn't let their circumstance define them. Most of them found a way to turn their setback into something greater than themselves, just as Chad did.

MORE WITH ONE ARM

You may remember the young surfer whose arm was bitten off by a shark, Bethany Hamilton. As I read her book Soul Surfer I was touched by her commitment to making a difference and not giving up. One of my favorite quotes from her that I often repeat to myself is, "I've had the chance to embrace more people with one arm than I ever have with two."[4] Do your experiences open you up to help more people? People want to connect with people they trust and believe in, who understand them and love them. Is that you? You never know who God may need you to help because of your unique perspective.

I think about all the good that Bethany and Chad are doing in the world and wonder where they would be if they had not embraced a positive perspective on their circumstances.

CHANGE OF PERSPECTIVE

In the movie made about her life, Soul Surfer, Bethany has a conversation with her Christian leader played by Carrie Underwood. Bethany reflects, "You know how you say that sometimes

3   Ibid.
4   Bethany Hamilton and Rick Bundschuh, Soul Surfer: A True
Story of Faith, Family, and Fighting to Get Back on the Board (New York:
Simon & Schuster, 2004)

we can't see things clearly because we are too close, that sometimes we just need a change of perspective?"[5]

Maybe you feel like you are up against a brick wall that seems
huge and insurmountable. If you took a few steps back and
looked at it again, would it still look the same? It has been my
experience that often our "huge brick wall" is more like a small
four-foot wall that we could easily walk around, or even climb
over with some concentrated effort.

When things seem overwhelming and you feel you may not be
able to face them, take a step back and gain a new perspective
on the situation. Make a gratitude list, ask for someone else's
view of the situation, or look at things from a different angle.
Ask yourself, "What good can come from this? What can I
learn?" Determine whether you really need to break the wall, or
scale it with climbing equipment? Ask yourself what you need
to do to get through the wall that is keeping you stuck. Is it really
a wall or merely a small stumbling block?

GUT CHECK

*Do you view your circumstances as
a learning opportunity? Are you
learning things that can bless others? Are you grateful for the experiences you are having? Do you need
to step back from the wall and gain a
new perspective?*

---

5   Soul Surfer (Film District and TriStar Pictures, 2011)

KEY # 9:

DEVELOP AN OUTWARD MINDSET

*"If you would win a man to your cause, first convince
him that you are his sincere friend."*
Abraham Lincoln

IS AN INWARD MINDSET STOPPING YOU

I want you to think for a minute. How do you see other people? What do you think when someone cuts you off in traffic? What is your gut reaction to a client who is late for an appointment? What about the neighbor with the dog that poops on your lawn and never cleans it up? Most likely you don't have warm fuzzy feelings for these people, right?

What if you were that person in someone else's life? How would you hope they view you? I would guess that if you really were any of these people, you weren't doing these things maliciously, right? You probably didn't even see the guy you cut off — that's why you cut him off. And you weren't disrespectful of others' time when you were late — you had an emergency that couldn't wait. And as for the dog? Maybe you don't even know your dog is doing his duty somewhere else.

So often we want people to see us as we are, as mortals. We make mistakes, we have a good heart, we have hopes and dreams, weaknesses and strengths. But how often do we fail to see others that way? We assume that they should have it all together. We tend to judge against an insurmountable scale that no one could ever reach. We don't even hold ourselves to that scale, yet we expect it from others. We judge others by their actions but we judge ourselves by our intentions.

People respond to how you feel about them on the inside. They can often see through even your best attempts to fake love and charity. Have you ever been around someone who you felt was just putting on an act to be nice to you? Maybe that individual was a good actor, but you could just feel it wasn't genuine.

Now, think of someone that you know loves you and with whom you always feel safe. What's the difference? The latter knows all about you, and still loves you unconditionally. But often it is common for the human race to love, serve, and be kind only conditionally.

Without realizing it we might be thinking, "I will love you as long as you do everything the way I want you to do it, make the decisions the way I would, and fit my expectations of you perfectly. If you don't, well then, good luck, because I only like people who are perfect."

Of course that sounds absurd, doesn't it? But too often it's reality. How often do you fall into that trap? If you really want to make a difference in your life and your business, you have to start seeing people through what I call an "outward mindset." Instead of "What do I benefit from this exchange?" Think "How can THEY benefit from an exchange with me?"

When you get so caught up in how you are going to make your next paycheck or who your next contact will be, you may lose sight of the gift you have to give to others. It's all about you at that point. And they can feel that.

My favorite book that illustrates this point beautifully is titled Leadership and Self Deception: Getting Out of the Box, by the Arbinger Institute. It tells the story of a man who assumes a leadership position in a new job and undergoes extensive training on how to be out of the box with his mindset. The character says, "I saw in myself a leader who was so sure of the brilliance of his own ideas that he couldn't allow brilliance in anyone else's; a leader who felt he was so 'enlightened' that he needed to see workers negatively in order to prove his enlightenment; a leader so driven to be the best that he made sure no one else could be as good as he was."[1]

When we fall into this kind of thinking, we assume that everything is about us and we lose sight of the people around us who could be blessed by us.

NOT JUST A NUMBER

Once a month I get the amazing opportunity to join with my fellow speakers at the National Speakers Association meeting. Each meeting is filled with wonderful training from the best speakers in the nation. Recently I had the opportunity to meet an amazing man who truly understands the outward mindset.

Patrick Henry is a singer/songwriter/speaker/humorist who helps businesses see the importance of realizing that their customers and employees are not just a number. He shared this poem with us that really touched me:

> I am not a number. I'm a person.
> I am not a number. I'm real.
> I have joy and hopes and sadness.
> I am not a number. I feel.

1   Arbinger Institute, Leadership and Self-Deception: Getting Out of the Box (Farmington UT: The Arbinger Institute, 2016)

I'm not the cancer in room 311
or the diabetic in 402.
I'm not the four top in the atrium
or the quaint 2 1/2 bath 3 bedroom.

I'm not the ADHD on the red hall,
Or the lowest test score on the blue.
I am not a number, I'm a person just like you.

I'm not a half percentage point or a margin call,
the sum of pounds read on a scale.
I'm not row 8 seat 32,
Or the commission on a sale.

I'm not a case to be managed,
I'm not the next in line.
I'm not a double decaf mocha latte
Or a 20-year term life.

I am not a number, I'm a person
And I demand your respect.
But if you treat me like a number,
Then a number's what you'll get.

A number won't stay loyal if there comes a better deal.
A number knows no allegiance because a number cannot
feel.
Be kind to me and I'll open my heart
Invite me in, and I'll eagerly take part.

Recognize my significance.
Celebrate my individuality.
Don't treat me like a number,
And you'll have my loyalty.

(To see Patrick tell this poem on stage go to
www.patrickhenryspeaker.com)[2]

An outward mindset means seeing people as they are, just like you, with hopes and dreams, weaknesses and strengths. It is letting go of judgement and letting people be who they are. It's not comparing, or making excuses. It is a true love that transcends mistakes, gender, race, and identity. It is seeing people as people, not as numbers.

SIT ON THE SAME SIDE OF THE TABLE

When we are always sitting on the same side of the table with our client, spouse, child, etc. it makes all the difference in the world.

What is sitting on the same side of the table? It's putting others best interest at the forefront. It's not about what you are going to from the interaction or how you can benefit from it, but what will really make a difference in their life. It is both of you coming up with a solution that really is the best fit for them, not you.

My husband and I work with many individuals who are addicted to pornography. We see this idea of sitting on the same side of the table become very important in the recovery process. Imagine the spouse of an addict. Initially, they may be so hurt and angry with the addict that they may not know how to respond. They see themselves and the addict sitting on opposite sides of the table, with God on one end trying to communicate and help each of them, and Satan on the other trying to destroy them. You can imagine how much headway toward recovery they make when they are in that space. But what if the spouse, the addict, and God were all sitting on the same side of the table, creating a united front against Satan who sat across the table? How much more effective could they be in breaking down the shame and finding recovery? It makes all the difference, but it has to start with the spouse seeing the addict as a person who makes mistakes and

2   Patrick Henry, "I am not a number" (www.patrickhenryspeaker. com)

wants to be better, not as someone who was ruining their life and trying to cause hurt or pain.

What about sitting on the same side of the table in your business dealings? Having an outward mindset means you are truly not in it for yourself. For example, sometimes that means *not* selling them something. If they don't really need what you have, then you are out of integrity selling it to them and you don't have an outward mindset towards them. You are looking at it from the inside saying "I need this.", whatever that may be.

That doesn't mean that you never benefit from the interaction. In fact, I believe that when you can truly come from the place of an outward mindset, you will be far more successful than if you are counting enrollees, or sales, or pushing numbers. Things will happen more organically. There is still place for numbers and strategy, but what I suggest is that you first make sure your heart and intent is in the right place in all of your dealings.

How do we develop an outward mindset? This is the golden question, and I'm not sure I have a clear answer for it. I pray for it. I practice it. I check myself often to see if I am looking at people as numbers or people. I try to imagine them as children of a loving creator who loves them as much as He loves me.

How would your business interactions change if you sat on the same side of the table with your client? What about your spouse? Or children?

WEAR GODLY GOGGLES

My husband listened as a man who was a hostage negotiator spoke of the process he went through to get hostages released. The man said the most important step was to gain a respect for the captor. Before each operation, he takes a picture of the captor, the one who is holding others hostage, and stares at the picture. He looks into the eyes of the person and tries to imagine what he might be like. He does this until he has gained respect for this person as an individual (not for his choices, but for him as a human being). He knows that without that respect and genuine caring for the captor, he doesn't stand a chance of working out a solution to get the hostages free. He claims that they can tell if you are just saying what they want to hear and don't really mean it.

If gaining respect for someone who is committing a huge crime and hurting others is so important, how much more important is it for us to gain the same respect for people in our lives?

Put on your Godly Goggles and see people the way God sees them, with hopes, dreams, strengths and weaknesses, fears and challenges.

I love what Marvin J. Ashton said about the outward mindset, or true charity:

Real charity is not something you give away; it is something that you acquire and make a part of yourself. And when the virtue of charity becomes implanted in your heart, you are never the same again...Perhaps the greatest charity comes when we are kind to each other, when we don't judge or categorize someone else, when we simply give each other the benefit of the doubt or remain quiet. Charity is accepting someone's differences, weaknesses, and shortcomings; having patience with someone who has let us down; or resisting the impulse to become offended when someone doesn't handle something the way we might have hoped. Charity is refusing to take advantage of another's weakness and being willing to forgive someone who has hurt us. Charity is expecting the best of each other. None of us needs one more person bashing or pointing out where we have failed or fallen short. Most of us are already well aware of the areas in which we are weak. What each of us does need is family, friends, employers, and brothers and sisters who support us, who have the patience to teach us, who believe in us, and who believe we're trying to do the best we can in spite of our weaknesses. Whatever happened to giving each other the benefit of the doubt? Whatever happened to hoping that another person would succeed or achieve? Whatever happened to rooting for each other?[3]

IT'S NOT ABOUT YOU

Chad Hymas taught me that in life, it's not about me, it's about them. And it's not just about them; it's about who they will bless because I blessed them.

I worked with a dietician a while back to try to balance out my blood sugar. She taught me a great little tip to help regulate my levels when I eat sugar. She taught me to always eat some protein or fat when I eat sugar. I tried it for a few days and it made a big difference. I shared the tip with my kids, then my mother-in-law,

3   Marvin J Ashton, "The Tongue Can Be a Sharp Sword," Ensign, May 1992

who then shared it with others. My daughter has been going around school telling her friends that they should eat an egg with their cookie. That one tip from someone who really wanted me to feel better, has impacted many lives. I have shared that tip with so many people I could never count them all.

When it comes to sharing what we know, it's not about what we can gain from sharing, it's about what others can gain and who they can bless because we shared with them. I love this quote from Jeffrey R. Holland, "I may not be my brother's keeper, but I am my brother's brother."[4]

4 Jeffrey R Holland, "Are We Not All Beggars," Ensign, Nov 2014, 40

GUT CHECK

I love this gut check from author and speaker Ty Bennett, in his book The Power of Influence. Take a moment to evaluate yourself.

1. In sales do you care more about A) the commission you make or B) the customer?

2. In leadership do you A) place blame or B) praise your people?

3. Do you A) feel threatened by the success of others or B) celebrate their triumphs?

4. In relationships do you A) try and change others or B) try to make yourself better?

5. In relationships do you A) want to win or B) do you want win-win?

6. When accidents happen do you respond A) with anger and annoyance or B) with care and concern?

7. When you are part of a team, do you concentrate A) on what you can do to excel individually or B) on what you can do to help the team excel?

8. If you're slicing a cake, do you give the largest piece to A) yourself or B) your companion?

9. In defeat do you A) make excuses and alibis or B) give credit to your opponent?

10. In social settings do you befriend the

loners and make people feel comfortable?

11. Do you give more compliments than you receive?

12. Do you keep score?[1]

After answering these questions, you can get a pretty good indication of where you fall on the outward mindset scale. What is one thing you can commit to doing right now that will move you closer to having an outward mindset as a habit?

---

1   Ty Bennett, The Power of Influence (American Fork, UT: Sound Concepts, Inc., 2013)

THE WRAP UP

Take a deep breath. You made it all the way to the end and you are still alive! For many people, swallowing all this information in one bite is overwhelming. Just start with one concept that stands out to you and work toward making one percent change in that area.

Dieter F. Uchtdorf shared what one degree difference can mean over time: "Suppose you were to take off from an airport at the equator, intending to circumnavigate the globe, but your course was off by just one degree. By the time you returned to the same longitude, how far off course would you be? A few miles? A hundred miles? The answer might surprise you. An error of only one degree would put you almost 500 miles (800 km) off course, or one hour of flight for a jet."[1]

Think about how much good can come from a one degree or one percent course correction over time. Every little change now will add up to huge change later. It all starts with one step!

And if you are afraid you don't have what it takes to change let me share with you the words of one of my favorite songs that I often sing when I speak or train:

---

1   Dieter F. Uchtdorf, "A Matter of a Few Degrees," Ensign, May 2008, 57.

"You Can Change"
by Tyler Castleton
www.tylercastleton.com

There are days
You stumble and you fall
And sometimes through it all
You think you'll never stand again

There are times
When choices weigh you down
And bend you to the ground
That's a place that we've all been

But you can change
You can turn your heart around
A brand new start can be found
If you'll only take one step

You can change
Wrap your mistakes in a cocoon
And let them die
And emerge a butterfly
You can change

Now it's time
To finally spread your wings
And soar to higher things
You know the limit is the sky

As you go
If you sometimes fail
When your spirit's frail
Remember you were [born] to fly

'Cause you can change
You can turn your heart around
A brand new start can be found
If you'll only take one step

You can change
Wrap your mistakes in a cocoon
And let them die
And emerge a butterfly
You can change

You can change
Wrap your mistakes in a cocoon
And let them die
And emerge a butterfly.[2]

As your coach, your cheerleader, and someone who wants you to quit faking happiness and truly love life, I invite you to change and pray that you will feel hope that change is possible. Remember, you were BORN TO FLY!

2   Tyler Castleton and Lowell Alexander, "You Can Change," (Diamond Aire Music 2009)

TESTIMONIALS

"Shelly's brilliant insight inspired me to change my own negative thoughts. She guides you with clarity to see how damaging these patterns can be in our daily lives. Her key principles have helped me reach goals in my life I never thought possible before."

-Krista, Idaho Falls, ID

"Shelly is amazing! She has helped me understand how my negative self-talk is blocking my goals and my life. I cannot wait to see where this journey takes me and my family and my team."

-Dawn, Rupert, ID

"Shelly's Master Your Mindset information is life-changing if you choose to apply it!"

-Tarilynn, Smithfield, UT

"Shelly awakened in me the motivation to change the way I was looking at difficulties in my life so I can make it through to the other side of them as a winner."

-Rebecca, Logan, UT

"I just completed Shelly's "Master Your Mindset" coaching course. During the six weeks I felt many changes happening in my life. My mindset shifted dramatically from vulnerable and victimized to being in control. It was a series of simple easy steps, simple daily changes to make to our lives that have a lasting effect. I highly recommend the program to anyone who is looking to make changes in their personal lives as well as in their business."

-Rayna, Columbia, MD

"Shelly is amazing. Her methods to retrain your brain are simple, yet so effective. She is a treasure."

-Kristy, West Jordan, UT

"I really connected with Shelly. What I took away was that I had control over my mind by training my subconscious and gaining confidence through the daily essentials and the nightly "ME" time. Now I am going to let my spirit be in charge so I can have control over my body."

-Torie, Logan, UT

ABOUT THE AUTHOR

Shelly Coray is a wife, mother, inspiring speaker, trainer, coach and author. She created the "Master Your Mindset" program to help individuals clear away the barriers that keep them from success. She is the founder of The Winner's Edge, a mental strength training program for youth, and the CEO of Rise Up International.

Through her 16 years involvement in high school athletics as a coach and manager and 20 years as an entrepreneur, Shelly has learned the keys to developing the mindset for success, making and breaking habits, and achieving peak performance. Among all the successes she helps people achieve, most of all she wants to help individuals become the person God created them to be.

Shelly resides with her husband and four children in Utah.

Shelly enjoys hearing from her readers. Reach out to her at Shelly@jimmyandshelly.com.